TEN TIMES BETTER

ALL RIGHTS RESERVED. YPLIFE
ALL SCRIPTURE QUOTATIONS ARE FROM THE KIN

COVER DESIGN: NICHOLAS WHITE
EDITING: JOHN M. SEAY

FOR ADDITIONAL COPIES OF *TEN TIMES BETTER* :

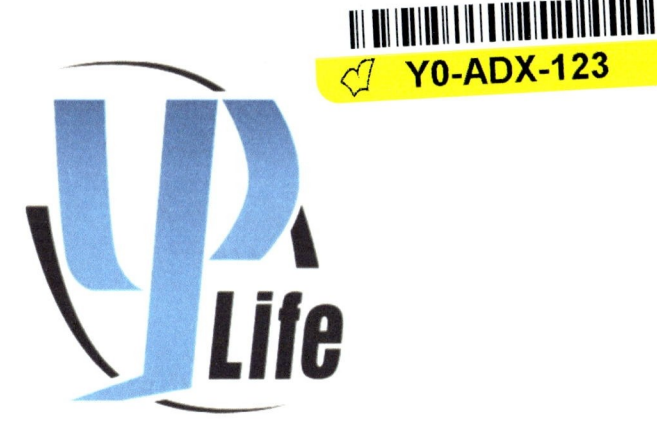

YPLIFE
3000 CLAYS MILL ROAD
LEXINGTON, KY 40503
(859) 321-2536
WWW.YPLIFE.ORG

PEOPLE THAT MADE THIS BOOK TEN TIMES BETTER

1. LORD JESUS CHRIST

2. JOHN M. SEAY

3. BIBIANN AVELAR

4. NICK WHITE

5. CALEB YOUNG

6. DEVIN OGDIE

7. ETHAN JACKSON

8. JONATHAN FUGATE

9. LUIS ROMERO

10. BRAD BRAUDIS

DEAR YOUNG PERSON,

ALL THROUGHOUT THE BIBLE WE ARE CHALLENGED TO BE BETTER, "GROW", "ADD", AND "LEARN". GOD WANTS US TO BECOME MORE LIKE HIM. BEING BETTER IS NOT ABOUT COMPETING WITH OTHER CHRISTIANS, BUT RATHER ABOUT BECOMING MORE LIKE CHRIST. BE BETTER THAN YOURSELF.
BE LIKE JESUS

TEN WAYS TO USE THIS BOOK

DEVOTIONS

ENJOY ENCOURAGING DEVOTIONS WRITTEN TO INSPIRE AND INSTRUCT YOU TO BE 10 TIMES BETTER.

HYMNS

READ THE STORIES BEHIND SOME OF THE MOST BELOVED HYMNS AS YOU SING PRAISES TO THE LORD.

BIBLE READING PLANS

FOLLOW ONE OF THE BIBLE READING PLANS.
1 CHAPTER A DAY, 3 CHAPTERS A DAY,
5 CHAPTERS A DAY, OR 10 CHAPTERS A DAY

PRAYER LIST

USE THE 7 DAY PRAYER LIST GUIDE TO HELP YOU PRAY EACH DAY.

SERMON NOTES

FILL 52 PAGES WITH NOTES FROM YOUR PASTOR AND YOUTH PASTOR.

TEN WAYS TO USE THIS BOOK

CALENDAR

A 12 MONTH PLANNER FOR BEING BETTER
ALL YEAR FOR CHRIST

CHAPTERS/VERSES

BIBLE CHAPTERS AND VERSES TO HELP
YOU BE 10 TIMES BETTER FOR CHRIST

CHARACTERS

READ THE STORIES OF CHARACTERS IN THE BIBLE
THAT WERE 10 TIMES BETTER FOR CHRIST.

STORIES

BIBLE STORIES OF 10 LEPERS, VIRGINS,
DAYS, SPIES, AND COMMANDMENTS

INSTRUCTIONS

LISTS COMPILED TO HELP YOU BE
BETTER IN EVERY AREA OF LIFE

-BE BETTER (PT. 1)-

DANIEL 1:20

Daniel 1:20, *"And in all matters of wisdom and understanding, that the king enquired of them, he found them ten times better than all the magicians and astrologers that were in all his realm."*

Daniel was captured and taken to a foriegn land. When challenged to accept the ways of the world, he refused and followed the Word of God in his heart. When the time came for Daniel to be tested, he was found ten times better than the people of the world. We as Christians should strive to be "ten times better" as well. Here is how you can be better:

1. TO BE BETTER WE MUST BE CLEAN.
Daniel 1:4 describes Daniel as being without blemish. When we think of a blemish, we think of makeup covering bad spot. To be without blemish is to be without spot. To be clean, holy, righteous. No question or blemish in our lives. Be better. Be clean.

2. TO BE BETTER WE MUST BE FRIENDLY.
In Daniel 1:4 the Bible says that Daniel was well-favored. In verse nine, the Bible says that God had brought Daniel into favour and tender love with the prince. It is false to believe that to be a good christian you have to be mean in your approach. You are not to be ugly in your postion or your dispostion. In your youth department you should be better. Be friendly.

3. TO BE BETTER WE MUST BE MATURE.
Daniel 1:4 says that Daniel had an ability to stand in the king's palace. For a young man to have the maturity to stand in the presence of royalty without wavering is an impressive feat. We should work to have that same maturity in our teen departments today. Everything should not be a joke and every day is not a activity. Learn to be sober minded and to work. Be better. Be mature.

4. TO BE BETTER WE MUST BE WILLING TO LEARN.
Not only did Daniel 1:4 tell us that Daniel was clean and friendly, it tells us that Daniel was skillful in all wisdom, cunning in knowledge, and understanding in science. This verse tells me that Daniel had a love for learning from a young age. You aren't born wise, you learn wisdom over time. You can choose to spend your life without ever enjoying learning, but you will never be better. Successful people are never satisfied with how much they know, they always want to learn more. If you will train yourself to love learning, you will be head and shoulders above others in all areas of life. You stop growing when you stop learning. Be better. Be willing to learn.

-BE BETTER (PT. 2)-

5. TO BE BETTER WE MUST BE PURPOSED.

Daniel 1:8 says, "But Daniel purposed in his heart that he would not defile himself with the portion of the king's meat." Purpose is having a plan and sticking with it. Many will make decisions at big events, such as camps and conferences, but those who keep the decisions, do so with purpose We must purpose in our hearts that we will do right. We must made the decision inside so that on the outside the decision is easy. We must purpose in our hearts that we will be better. Be better. Be purposed.

6. TO BE BETTER WE MUST BE WILLING TO SACRIFICE.

Daniel was given the opportunity to have everything desirable. The king's meat, the king's drink, and the king's care were all given to Daniel if he wanted. Though these things seem great, Daniel knew that to accept these provisions, would be turning his back on his home and his God. He purposed that he would sacrifice the king's meat and drink to rely wholly on God. After being proven ten days, Daniel was found 10 times better. When you sacrifice your dreams and desires to trust fully on God, you will find God's will to be ten times better. Be better. Be willing to sacrifice.

7. TO BE BETTER WE MUST NOT QUIT.

Daniel 1:21 says "And Daniel continued..." Daniel was given ample opportunities to give up, but he continued. The Bible is full of men that had opportunities to throw in the towel, but decided they were going to finish the race. Success and failure are separated by one word, "quit". From the kings meat, to the lions den, Daniel overcame trials and testing by determining that no matter how hard the circumstance, he would not quit. There may have been many hebrew boys eating meat and bowing down but not Daniel. He was not a quitter. Be better. Dont quit.

8. TO BE BETTER WE MUST GIVE GOD THE GLORY.

Daniel interprets the King's dream that no one could interpret. God had given Daniel the wisdom and insight to the dream and its interpretation and instead of exclaiming his own wisdom, Daniel spends four verses proclaiming praises unto God. Daniel would be exalted but would never place his own glorification above God's. To be better, we must cease from self-glorification, and recognize God is the reason for our success. Without HIm we can do nothing.
Be better. Give God the Glory.

WEEK

SUN.		PSALM 1
MON.		PSALM 2
TUES.		PSALM 3
WED.		PSALM 4
THURS.		PSALM 5
FRI.		PSALM 6
SAT.		PSALM 7

SUN.	GEN. 1-2	MATT. 1
MON.	GEN. 3-4	MATT. 2
TUES.	GEN. 5-6	MATT. 3
WED.	GEN. 7-8	MATT. 4
THURS.	GEN. 9-10	MATT. 5
FRI.	GEN. 11-12	MATT. 6
SAT.	GEN. 13-14	MATT. 7

TEN × BETTER — 1

SUN.	GEN. 1-3	MATT. 1-2
MON.	GEN. 4-6	MATT. 3-4
TUES.	GEN. 7-9	MATT. 5-6
WED.	GEN. 10-12	MATT. 7-8
THURS.	GEN. 13-15	MATT. 9-10
FRI.	GEN. 16-18	MATT. 11-12
SAT.	GEN. 19-21	MATT. 13-14

SUN.	GEN. 1-6	MATT. 1-4
MON.	GEN. 7-12	MATT. 5-8
TUES.	GEN. 13-18	MATT. 9-12
WED.	GEN. 19-24	MATT. 13-16
THURS.	GEN 25-30	MATT. 17-20
FRI.	GEN 31-36	MATT. 21-24
SAT.	GEN 37-42	MATT. 25-28

WEEK 1

SUN.		PSALM 8
MON.		PSALM 9
TUES.		PSALM 10
WED.		PSALM 11
THURS.		PSALM 12
FRI.		PSALM 13
SAT.		PSALM 14

SUN.	GEN. 15-16	MATT. 8
MON.	GEN. 17-18	MATT. 9
TUES.	GEN. 19-20	MATT. 10
WED.	GEN. 21-22	MATT. 11
THURS.	GEN. 23-24	MATT. 12
FRI.	GEN. 25-26	MATT. 13
SAT.	GEN. 27-28	MATT. 14

WEEK 2 — TEN TIMES BETTER

SUN.	GEN. 22-24	MATT. 15-16
MON.	GEN. 25-27	MATT. 17-18
TUES.	GEN. 28-30	MATT. 19-20
WED.	GEN. 31-33	MATT. 21-22
THURS.	GEN. 34-36	MATT. 23-24
FRI.	GEN. 37-39	MATT. 25-26
SAT.	GEN. 40-42	MATT. 27-28

SUN.	GEN. 43-48	MARK 1-4
MON.	GEN. 49 - EX. 4	MARK 5-8
TUES.	EX. 5-10	MARK 9-12
WED.	EX. 11-16	MARK 13-16
THURS.	EX. 17-22	LUKE 1-4
FRI.	EX. 23-28	LUKE 5-8
SAT.	EX. 29-34	LUKE 9-12

WEEK 3 — TEN X BETTER

SUN.	PSALM 15		SUN.	GEN. 29-30	MATT. 15
MON.	PSALM 16		MON.	GEN. 31-32	MATT. 16
TUES.	PSALM 17		TUES.	GEN. 33-34	MATT. 17
WED.	PSALM 18		WED.	GEN. 35-36	MATT. 18
THURS.	PSALM 19		THURS.	GEN. 37-38	MATT. 19
FRI.	PSALM 20		FRI.	GEN. 39-40	MATT. 20
SAT.	PSALM 21		SAT.	GEN. 41-42	MATT. 21

SUN.	GEN. 43-45	MARK 1-2	SUN.	EXO. 35-40	LUKE 13-16
MON.	GEN. 46-48	MARK 3-4	MON.	LEV. 1-6	LUKE 17-20
TUES.	GEN. 49 - EX. 1	MARK 5-6	TUES.	LEV. 7-12	LUKE 21-24
WED.	EX. 2-4	MARK 7-8	WED.	LEV. 13-18	JOHN 1-4
THURS.	EX. 5-7	MARK 9-10	THURS.	LEV. 19-24	JOHN 5-8
FRI.	EX. 8-10	MARK 11-12	FRI.	LEV. 25 - NUM. 3	JOHN 9-12
SAT.	EX. 11-13	MARK 13-14	SAT.	NUM. 4-9	JOHN 13-16

TEN TIMES BETTER

WEEK 4 — TEN X BETTER

SUN.	PSALM 22	GEN. 43-44	SUN.	MATT. 22
MON.	PSALM 23	GEN. 45-46	MON.	MATT. 23
TUES.	PSALM 24	GEN. 47-48	TUES.	MATT. 24
WED.	PSALM 25	GEN. 49-50	WED.	MATT. 25
THURS.	PSALM 26	EX. 1-2	THURS.	MATT. 26
FRI.	PSALM 27	EX. 3-4	FRI.	MATT. 27
SAT.	PSALM 28	EX. 5-6	SAT.	MATT. 28

SUN.	EX. 14-16	MARK 15-16	SUN.	NUM. 10-15	JOHN 17-20
MON.	EX. 17-19	LUKE 1-2	MON.	NUM. 16-21	JOHN 21 - ACTS 3
TUES.	EX. 20-22	LUKE 3-4	TUES.	NUM. 22-27	ACTS 4-7
WED.	EX. 23-25	LUKE 5-6	WED.	NUM. 28-33	ACTS 8-11
THURS.	EX. 26-28	LUKE 7-8	THURS.	NUM. 34 - DEUT. 3	ACTS 12-15
FRI.	EX. 29-31	LUKE 9-10	FRI.	DEUT. 4-9	ACTS 16-19
SAT.	EX. 32-34	LUKE 11-12	SAT.	DEUT. 10-15	ACTS 20-23

TEN TIMES BETTER

X WAYS TO BE A BETTER BUS WORKER

1. DESIGNATED BUS PRAYER TIMES
2. KNOCK AT LEAST 10 EXTRA DOORS
3. SPEND 20 MINUTES AT 1 HOME THIS WEEK
4. SMILE
5. SET TARGETS
6. CARRY TREATS
7. TAKE SOMEONE OUT THAT IS NEW VISITING
8. LEARN A NEW SONG
9. WRITE DOWN YOUR BUS PROGRAM
10. USE VISUAL AIDS

-Steve Johnson

> **FAITH IS THE WILLINGNESS TO RISK ANYTHING ON GOD.**
>
> **JACK HYLES**

-BE BETTER (PT. 3)-

9. TO BE BETTER WE MUST BE ALWAYS LIVING BY FAITH.

Daniel 3 gives us the account of the fiery furnace. King Nebuchadnezzar made the prideful decree that when the music plays, everyone was to bow down and worship the golden image of himself. He proclaimed that any man that would not bow would be cast into a burning fiery furnace. Three Jewish boys, Shadrach, Meshach, and Abednego would not bow to the wicked king's commands, but rather chose to be thrown in the furnace. They said that they trust the Lord would deliver them even from such extreme measures. The three Jewish boys would come out of the fire unharmed. We are going to be faced with "fire" in our lives, and the only thing that will get us through will be our continuous faith in God. When we place our faith in Him fire, He stands in the fire with us. Be Better. Live by Faith.

10. TO BE BETTER WE MUST BE CONSISTENT.

Daniel 6 tells us about the consistency of Daniel's walk with God. The King had signed a decree that noone could pray. Daniel didn't let man's decree discourage him from his walk with God. The Bible says he went to his room and opened his windows, just as he did aforetime, and prayed. When the wicked men saw Daniel praying, they immediately told the king. The king the commanded that he be thrown into the lion's den. Daniel's faith in God was so strong that the king himself said, "Thy God whom thou servest continually, he will deliver thee." God sent an angel to shut the mouths of the lions that would have otherwise been the death of Daniel. Daniel was delivered from the den of lions. In our walk with God, we face a roaring lion that walks about trying to devour us, but by being an every day Christian, we can shut the mouths of those lions. We can make a difference in the wicked world we live in by simply being "Christ-like" every day. Be consistent. Pray everyday, read everyday, witness everyday. Just be better every day... be consistently better.

-William Davis

✘ QUESTIONS FOR BETTER DECISIONS

1. AM I WILLING TO DO WHAT IS RIGHT ONCE I KNOW GOD'S WILL?
2. DO THE BEST CHRISTIANS I KNOW AGREE WITH THIS DECISION?
3. DOES MY DECISION AGREE WITH ALL THAT THE SCRIPTURE HAS TO SAY?
4. DO I HAVE THE LEADING OF THE HOLY SPIRIT?
5. DOES THE DECISION I'M ABOUT TO MAKE PLEASE GOD?
6. CAN I DO IT IN THE NAME OF THE LORD JESUS?
7. IF I DO THIS WILL IT DISHONOR GOD?
8. WOULD THIS DECISION OFFEND MY BROTHER IN CHRIST OR CAUSE OTHERS TO SIN?
9. AM I FULLY PERSUADED THAT I'M MAKING THE RIGHT DECISION?
10. HAVE I PRAYED ABOUT IT?

-Mark Eaton

✗ REASONS TO READ THE BIBLE

1. TO HELP US UNDERSTAND LIFE
For the commandment is a lamp; and the law is light; and reproofs of instruction are the way of life: **(Proverbs 6:23)**

2. TO NOT SIN
Wherewithal shall a young man cleanse his way? by taking heed thereto according to thy word. **(Psalm 119:9)**

3. TO BE ABLE TO CATCH FALSE TEACHING
Beloved, believe not every spirit, but try the spirits whether they are of God: because many false prophets are gone out into the world. **(1 John 4:1)**

4. TO GAIN A HUNGER FOR GOD
As newborn babes, desire the sincere milk of the word, that ye may grow thereby: **(1 Peter 2:2)**

5. TO ENCOURAGE US
For whatsoever things were written aforetime were written for our learning, that we through patience and comfort of the scriptures might have hope. **(Romans 15:4)**

6. FOR BETTER FELLOWSHIP WITH BELIEVERS
But if we walk in the light, as he is in the light, we have fellowship one with another... **(1 John 1:7a)**

7. TO DEFEND THE FAITH
But sanctify the Lord God in your hearts: and be ready always to give an answer to every man that asketh you a reason of the hope that is in you with meekness and fear: **(1 Peter 3:15)**

8. TO HAVE A WHOLE-HEARTED FAITH
Give me understanding, and I shall keep thy law; yea, I shall observe it with my whole heart. **(Psalm 119:34)**

9. TO HAVE MORE HOPE
And take not the word of truth utterly out of my mouth; for I have hoped in thy judgments. **(Psalm 119:43)**

10. IT WAS GIVEN BY GOD
All scripture is given by inspiration of God, and is profitable for doctrine, for reproof, for correction, for instruction in righteousness: **(2 Timothy 3:16)**

-✘ WAYS TO FIND A WALK WITH GOD-

JOSHUA 1:8, PSALMS 1:1-3

Joshua 1:8 talks about "good success". Psalm 1 speaks of being blessed, delighting, being planted, bringing fruit, not withering and prospering. Everyone wants a life like this. For the Christian a life like this begins with our walk with God. We have heard it 100 times... but how can we find a walk with God?

1. Find Your Bible- You may have 3 Bibles but find you one specific Bible to read and study from.

2. Find a Place- Pick a room, a seat or a location to read and pray every day.

3. Find a Time- The Psalmist said morning, evening. Maybe after school, before school, on way to school, before bed or when you wake up..

4. Find a Plan- Use a Bible reading calendar or schedule that works for you.

5. Find Some Helping Tools- A Concordance, Pen, Notebook, highlighter, books, music, notes in church all are helps in walking with God.

6. Find a Way to Eliminate Distractions- Many times People, Phones, TV, Tasks and other things can distract us from our walk.

7. Find Time to Pray- When you read the Bible find time to add Prayer to your devotions.

8. Find Joy in the Relationship- God is not just about the Rules and Religion. He's about the Relationship. It's not just about the 3 chapters, it's about the God who wrote them.

9. Find Goals and Desires- Get something out of what you read. How can you apply what you found in the Bible.

10. Find the Holy Spirit- Meditate. Fellowship with the third part of the Godhead that lives inside of you.

FIND A WAY TO WALK WITH GOD EVERY DAY!   *-William Davis*

TEN X BETTER

WEEK 5

SUN.	PSALM 29		SUN.	EX. 7-8	MARK 1
MON.	PSALM 30		MON.	EX. 9-10	MARK 2
TUES.	PSALM 31		TUES.	EX. 11-12	MARK 3
WED.	PSALM 32		WED.	EX. 13-14	MARK 4
THURS.	PSALM 33		THURS.	EX. 15-16	MARK 5
FRI.	PSALM 34		FRI.	EX. 17-18	MARK 6
SAT.	PSALM 35		SAT.	EX. 19-20	MARK 7

SUN.	EX. 35-37	LUKE 13-14	SUN.	DEUT. 16-21	ACTS 24-27
MON.	EX. 38-40	LUKE 15-16	MON.	DEUT. 22-27	ACTS 28 - ROM. 3
TUES.	LEV. 1-3	LUKE 17-18	TUES.	DEUT. 28-33	ROM. 4-7
WED.	LEV. 4-6	LUKE 19-20	WED.	DEUT. 34 - JOSH. 5	ROM. 8-11
THURS.	LEV. 7-9	LUKE 21-22	THURS.	JOSH. 6-11	ROM. 12-15
FRI.	LEV. 10-12	LUKE 23-24	FRI.	JOSH. 12-17	ROM. 16 - 1 COR. 3
SAT.	LEV. 13-15	JOHN 1-2	SAT.	JOSH. 18-23	1 CORIN. 4-7

WEEK 6

TEN

SUN.	PSALM 36	
MON.	PSALM 37	
TUES.	PSALM 38	
WED.	PSALM 39	
THURS.	PSALM 40	
FRI.	PSALM 41	
SAT.	PSALM 42	

SUN.	LEV. 16-18	JOHN 3-4
MON.	LEV. 19-21	JOHN 5-6
TUES.	LEV. 22-24	JOHN 7-8
WED.	LEV. 25-27	JOHN 9-10
THURS.	NUM. 1-3	JOHN 11-12
FRI.	NUM. 4-6	JOHN 13-14
SAT.	NUM. 7-9	JOHN 15-16

TIMES BETTER

SUN.	EX. 21-22	MARK 8
MON.	EX. 23-24	MARK 9
TUES.	EX. 25-26	MARK 10
WED.	EX. 27-28	MARK 11
THURS.	EX. 29-30	MARK 12
FRI.	EX. 31-32	MARK 13
SAT.	EX. 33-34	MARK 14

SUN.	JOSH. 24 - JUDG. 5	1 COR. 8-11
MON.	JUDG. 6-11	1 COR. 12-15
TUES.	JUDG. 12-17	1 COR. 16 - 2 COR. 3
WED.	JUDG. 18 - RUTH 2	2 COR. 4-7
THURS.	RUTH 3 - 1 SAM. 4	2 COR. 8-11
FRI.	1 SAM. 5-10	2 COR. 12 - GAL. 2
SAT.	1 SAM. 11-16	GAL. 3-6

WEEK 7

TEN

SUN.	PSALM 43	NUM. 10-12
MON.	PSALM 44	NUM. 13-15
TUES.	PSALM 45	NUM. 16-18
WED.	PSALM 46	NUM. 19-21
THURS.	PSALM 47	NUM. 22-24
FRI.	PSALM 48	NUM. 25-27
SAT.	PSALM 49	NUM. 28-30

SUN.	JOHN 17-18
MON.	JOHN 19-20
TUES.	JOHN 21 - ACTS 1
WED.	ACTS 2-3
THURS.	ACTS 4-5
FRI.	ACTS 6-7
SAT.	ACTS 8-9

BETTER

SUN.	EX. 35-36	MARK 15
MON.	EX. 37-38	MARK 16
TUES.	EX. 39-40	LUKE 1
WED.	NUM. 1-2	LUKE 2
THURS.	NUM. 3-4	LUKE 3
FRI.	NUM. 5-6	LUKE 4
SAT.	NUM. 7-8	LUKE 5

SUN.	1 SAM. 17-22	EPH. 1-4
MON.	1 SAM. 23-28	EPH. 5 - PHIL. 2
TUES.	1 SAM. 29 - 2 SAM. 3	PHIL. 3 - COLO. 2
WED.	2 SAM. 4-9	COLO. 3 - 1 THES. 2
THURS.	2 SAM. 10-15	1 THES. 3 - 2 THES. 1
FRI.	2 SAM. 16-21	2 THES. 2 - 1 TIM. 2
SAT.	2 SAM. 22 - 1 KINGS 3	1 TIM. 3-6

WEEK 8

TEN

SUN.		PSALM 50
MON.		PSALM 51
TUES.		PSALM 52
WED.		PSALM 53
THURS.		PSALM 54
FRI.		PSALM 55
SAT.		PSALM 56

SUN.	NUM. 31-33	ACTS 10-11
MON.	NUM. 34-36	ACTS 12-13
TUES.	DEUT. 1-3	ACTS 14-15
WED.	DEUT. 4-6	ACTS 16-17
THURS.	DEUT. 7-9	ACTS 18-19
FRI.	DEUT. 10-12	ACTS 20-21
SAT.	DEUT. 13-15	ACTS 22-23

BETTER

SUN.	NUM. 9-10	LUKE 6
MON.	NUM. 11-12	LUKE 7
TUES.	NUM. 13-14	LUKE 8
WED.	NUM. 15-16	LUKE 9
THURS.	NUM. 17-18	LUKE 10
FRI.	NUM. 19-20	LUKE 11
SAT.	NUM. 21-22	LUKE 12

SUN.	1 KINGS 4-9	2 TIM. 1-4
MON.	1 KINGS 10-15	TITUS - PHM.
TUES.	1 KINGS 16-21	HEB. 1-4
WED.	1 KINGS 22 - 2 KINGS 5	HEB. 5-8
THURS.	2 KINGS 6-11	HEB. 9-12
FRI.	2 KINGS 12-17	HEB. 13 - JAS. 3
SAT.	2 KINGS 18-23	JAS. 4 - 1 PET. 2

TEN TIMES BETTER

X WAYS TO HAVE A BETTER PRAYER LIFE

1. **MAKE A LIST**
2. **HAVE A TIME**
3. **HAVE A PLACE**
4. **BE SPECIFIC**
5. **PRAY EXPECTING**
6. **PRAISE GOD**
7. **REMEMBER OTHERS**
8. **PRAY ASKING**
9. **WRITE DOWN ANSWERS TO PRAYER**
10. **YIELD TO GOD'S WILL**

-William Davis

> **WHAT YOU DO WITH THE BIBLE DETERMINES WHAT GOD DOES WITH YOU.**
>
> — WILLIAM DAVIS

Be Thou My Vision

Dallan Forgaill
arranged by Eleanor H. Hull

1. Be Thou my Vi - sion, O Lord of my heart; Naught be all else to me, save that Thou art; Thou my best Thought, by day or by night, Wak - ing or sleep - ing, Thy pres-ence my light.
2. Be Thou my Wis - dom, and Thou my true Word; I ev - er with Thee and Thou with me, Lord; Thou my great Fa - ther, I Thy true son; Thou in me dwell - ing, and I with Thee one.
3. Be Thou my bat - tle Shield, Sword for the fight; Be Thou my Dig - ni - ty, Thou my De - light; Thou my soul's Shel - ter, Thou my high Tow'r: Raise Thou me heav'n-ward, O Pow'r of my pow'r.
4. Rich - es I heed not, nor man's emp-ty praise, Thou mine In - her - i - tance, now and al - ways: Thou and Thou on - ly, first in my heart, High King of Heav - en, my Treas-ure Thou art.
5. High King of Heav - en, my vic - to - ry won, May I reach Heav -en's joys, O bright Heav'n's Sun! Heart of my own heart, what-e'er be - fall, Still be my Vi - sion, O Rul - er of all.

BE THOU MY VISION

Only one missionary is honored with a global holiday, and only one is known by his own distinct color of green – St. Patrick missionary to Ireland. Patrick was born in Scotland, AD 385. When Patrick was about 16, raiders descended on his little town and torched his home. When one of the pirates spotted him, seized him, hauled aboard ship, and took him to Ireland as a slave. There he gave his life to the Lord Jesus. "The Lord opened my mind to an awareness of my unbelief." He later wrote," in order that I might remember my transgressions and turn with all my heart to the Lord my God." Patrick eventually escaped and returned home. His overjoyed family begged him to never leave again. One night, in a dream reminiscent of Paul's vision of the Macedonian man in Acts 16, Patrick saw an Irishman pleading with him to come evangelize Ireland. It wasn't an easy decision, but Patrick returned to his former captors with only one book in his hand, the Bible. As he evangelized the countryside, multitudes came to listen. The superstitious Druids opposed him and sought his death, but his preaching was powerful.

Patrick became one of the most fruitful evangelists of all time, planting about 200 churches and baptizing 100,000 converts. His work endured, and several centuries later, the Irish church was still producing hymns, prayers, sermons, and songs of worship.

In the eighth century, an unknown poet wrote a prayer asking God to be his Vision, his Wisdom, and his Best Thought by day or night. In 1905, Mary Elizabeth Byrne, a scholar in Dublin, Ireland, translated this ancient Irish poem into English. Another scholar, Eleanor Hull of Manchester, England, took Byrne's translation and crafted it into verses with rhyme and meter. Shortly thereafter it was set to a traditional Irish folk song, "Slane," named for an area in Ireland where Patrick reportedly challenged local Druids with the gospel. It is one of our oldest and most moving hymns.

-THE HEART OF THE MATTER-

PROVERBS 23:26 *"My son, give me thine heart..."*

We serve a God that is all sufficient. He is in and of himself sufficient. God does not have any needs at all. He owns all things. He created all things. By him, all things consist. God does not have needs so I cannot meet his needs, but I do believe God has a want. I am convinced that there is something that God desires. There is something that God longs for and I can provide it for him! God meets my needs. He puts food on my table and clothes on my back. He provides for my family and gives my body it's life. He meets my needs faithfully. I cannot meet God's needs, because he does not have any, however I can meet God's want! It is clear in this Proverb that the Father desires the heart of the son. Notice that there was already a relationship. He was already the father, but he desired more than to have a son, he wanted to have the heart of his son!

I believe we can make application here. I am convinced that God wants my heart. He wants my desire and my dreams. He wants my aspirations and my thoughts. He wants my devotion and my love. It is interesting that the father did not ask for the son's hands or his feet or his eyes or his ears or his tongue. I believe the father new that if he truly had the son's heart, the rest of the son would come in the package. If the father had his son's heart he'd have a better son.

May we not be quick to declare our hands for God or our feet for his service and neglect to offer God what he wants the most! The best gift we can offer God is--our heart!

> *"Take my will and make it Thine,*
> *It shall be no longer mine.*
> *Take my heart, it is Thine own,*
> *It shall be Thy royal throne."*

-Justin Cooper

✗ COMMANDMENTS

DEUTERONOMY 4:13-16a

"And he declared unto you his covenant, which he commanded you to perform, even ten commandments; and he wrote them upon two tables of stone. And the LORD commanded me at that time to teach you statutes and judgments, that ye might do them in the land whither ye go over to possess it. Take ye therefore good heed unto yourselves; for ye saw no manner of similitude on the day that the LORD spake unto you in Horeb out of the midst of the fire: Lest ye corrupt yourselves..."

God has rules that He wants us to follow. He has proclaimed these rules in His Word. Many times we ignore these rules and instead do what we want to do. We begin to justify our actions in our mind by saying, "The rules are there so stirct that I can't have any fun." This is the exact opposite of what God wants. He wants us to enjoy life, therefore He has in place rules for us to follow. God doesn't want our lives to be miserable. God said in verse 16 that the rules were set not to punish the children of Israel, but to keep them from corruption. God cared about His children then, and He most certainly cares about His children today. Young person, don't try to buck the rules and live in rebellion. The Devil is trying to destroy your life, but God is trying to preserve it. Make the decision today to live by the rules your authorities and ultimately God have set up in your life.

WEEK 9

TEN

SUN.	PSALM 57	ACTS 24-25
MON.	PSALM 58	ACTS 26-27
TUES.	PSALM 59	ACTS 28 - ROM. 1
WED.	PSALM 60	ROM. 2-3
THURS.	PSALM 61	ROM. 4-5
FRI.	PSALM 62	ROM. 6-7
SAT.	PSALM 63	ROM. 8-9

SUN.	DEUT. 16-18	
MON.	DEUT. 19-21	
TUES.	DEUT. 22-24	
WED.	DEUT. 25-27	
THURS.	DEUT. 28-30	
FRI.	DEUT. 31-33	
SAT.	DEUT. 34 - JOSH. 2	

BETTER

SUN.	NUM. 23-24	
MON.	NUM. 25-26	
TUES.	NUM. 27-28	
WED.	NUM. 29-30	
THURS.	NUM. 31-32	LUKE 17
FRI.	NUM. 33-34	LUKE 18
SAT.	NUM. 35-36	LUKE 19

SUN.	2 KINGS 24 - 1 CHR. 4	1 PET. 3 - 2 PET. 1
MON.	1 CHR. 5-10	2 PET. 2 - 1 JHN. 2
TUES.	1 CHR. 11-16	1 JHN. 3 - 2 JHN.
WED.	1 CHR. 17-22	3 JHN. REV. 2
THURS.	1 CHR. 23-28	REV. 3-6
FRI.	1 CHR. 29 - 2 CHR. 5	REV. 7-10
SAT.	2 CHR. 6-11	REV. 11-14

TEN TIMES BETTER

WEEK 10 — TEN X BETTER

SUN.	PSALM 64		SUN.	DEUT. 1-2	LUKE 20
MON.	PSALM 65		MON.	DEUT. 3-4	LUKE 21
TUES.	PSALM 66		TUES.	DEUT. 5-6	LUKE 22
WED.	PSALM 67		WED.	DEUT. 7-8	LUKE 23
THURS.	PSALM 68		THURS.	DEUT. 9-10	LUKE 24
FRI.	PSALM 69		FRI.	DEUT. 11-12	JOHN 1
SAT.	PSALM 70		SAT.	DEUT. 13-14	JOHN 2

SUN.	JOSH. 3-5	ROM. 10-11	SUN.	2 CHR. 12-17	REV. 15-18
MON.	JOSH. 6-8	ROM. 12-13	MON.	2 CHR. 18-23	REV. 19-22
TUES.	JOSH. 9-11	ROM. 14-15	TUES.	2 CHR. 24-29	MATT. 1-4
WED.	JOSH. 12-14	ROM. 16 - 1 COR. 1	WED.	2 CHR. 30-35	MATT. 5-8
THURS.	JOSH. 15-17	1 COR. 2-3	THURS.	2 CHR. 36 - EZRA 5	MATT. 9-12
FRI.	JOSH. 18-20	1 COR. 4-5	FRI.	EZRA 6 - NEH. 1	MATT. 13-16
SAT.	JOSH. 21-23	1 COR. 6-7	SAT.	NEH. 2-7	MATT. 17-20

WEEK

SUN.	PSALM 71	
MON.	PSALM 72	
TUES.	PSALM 73	
WED.	PSALM 74	
THURS.	PSALM 75	
FRI.	PSALM 76	
SAT.	PSALM 77	

SUN.	DEUT. 15-16	JOHN 3
MON.	DEUT. 17-18	JOHN 4
TUES.	DEUT. 19-20	JOHN 5
WED.	DEUT. 21-22	JOHN 6
THURS.	DEUT. 23-24	JOHN 7
FRI.	DEUT. 25-26	JOHN 8
SAT.	DEUT. 27-28	JOHN 9

TEN X BETTER — 11

TEN TIMES BETTER

SUN.	JOSH. 24 - JUDG. 2	1 CORIN. 8-9
MON.	JUDG. 3-5	1 CORIN. 10-11
TUES.	JUDG. 6-8	1 CORIN. 12-13
WED.	JUDG. 9-11	1 CORIN. 14-15
THURS.	JUDG. 12-14	1 CORIN. 16 - 2 CORIN. 1
FRI.	JUDG. 15-17	2 CORIN. 2-3
SAT.	JUDG. 18-20	2 CORIN. 4-5

SUN.	NEH. 8-13	MATT. 21-24
MON.	ESTH. 1-6	MATT. 25-28
TUES.	ESTH. 7 - JOB 2	MARK 1-4
WED.	JOB 3-8	MARK 5-8
THURS.	JOB 9-14	MARK 9-12
FRI.	JOB 15-20	MARK 13-16
SAT.	JOB 21-26	LUKE 1-4

TEN X BETTER — WEEK 12

SUN.	PSALM 78
MON.	PSALM 79
TUES.	PSALM 80
WED.	PSALM 81
THURS.	PSALM 82
FRI.	PSALM 83
SAT.	PSALM 84

SUN.	DEUT. 29-30
MON.	DEUT. 31-32
TUES.	DEUT. 33-34
WED.	JOSH. 1-2
THURS.	JOSH. 3-4
FRI.	JOSH. 5-6
SAT.	JOSH. 7-8

SUN.	JOHN 10
MON.	JOHN 11
TUES.	JOHN 12
WED.	JOHN 13
THURS.	JOHN 14
FRI.	JOHN 15
SAT.	JOHN 16

SUN.	JUDG. 21 - RUTH 2	2 COR. 6-7
MON.	RUTH 3 - 1 SAM. 1	2 COR. 8-9
TUES.	1 SAM. 2-4	2 COR. 10-11
WED.	1 SAM. 5-7	2 COR. 12-13
THURS.	1 SAM. 8-10	GAL. 1-2
FRI.	1 SAM. 11-13	GAL. 3-4
SAT.	1 SAM. 14-16	GAL. 5-6

SUN.	JOB 27-32	LUKE 5-8
MON.	JOB 33-38	LUKE 9-12
TUES.	JOB 39 - PSA. 2	LUKE 13-16
WED.	PSA. 3-8	LUKE 17-20
THURS.	PSA. 9-14	LUKE 21-24
FRI.	PSA. 15-20	JOHN 1-4
SAT.	PSA. 21-26	JOHN 5-8

TEN TIMES BETTER

X WAYS TO BE A BETTER SOUL WINNER

1. CARRY TRACTS
2. GIVE TRACTS
3. BE SOUL CONSCIENCE
4. SEE SOULS
5. LOVE PEOPLE
6. GO SOUL WINNING
7. PRAY FOR THE LOST
8. BE PREPARED
9. CARRY A NEW TESTAMENT
10. BE POLITE

-Flynn Rodgers/ Steve Fisher

> **CHARACTER IS WHAT YOU ARE IN THE DARK.**
>
> — D.L. MOODY

-FRUIT FROM CANAAN-

NUMBERS 13:20 *"And be ye of good courage and bring fruit of the land...."*

Everyone will have faith in something. The Bible shows us that faith comes from hearing; henceforth, we must be careful to what we listen to. Twelve spies came back from Canaan. Ten of them came back with an evil report. Notice the Bible does not say their report was inaccurate, but that their report was an evil report. Their report was accurate for there were giants in the land, walls around the land, and people stronger than they were. Their report was evil because their report lacked faith in God. Because of this evil report the people murmured against God. There were also two other spies that came back from Canaan land with a report to give the people. The two spies were Caleb and Joshua. Caleb came back and stilled the people saying that they could do what God had told them they could do and go into Canaan. The people did not listen to the Caleb, and as a result a whole generation dies in the wilderness.

Who are you listening to? Be careful who you are listening to, for faith comes by hearing. Although it is concerning that we may hear more of the bad news than the good news. Thank God for Caleb and Joshua and their report. Not everybody believed the ten spies. Even though they were in the minority they still sounded out the truth. Caleb did not just sound out the truth of Canaan. He brought back a sample of Canaan. He brought back some fruit from Canaan which the Bible said they had to have two men to cary the grapes. There must be folks who get up in the morning and go down to Canaan to bring back some fruit to their family. Someone who can bring back the fruit of answered prayer, peace, and joy. We need to keep stepping out in faith. It's not a matter of what we have, it's a matter of who we follow. Fear of losing causes us to lose what God wants us to have, which is better than what we have now. I don't want to be satisfied, there is a generation coming up behind me that needs to know the touch and taste of God. A taste of Canaan!

-Pastor Jeff Fugate

X DAYS

DANIEL 1:11-20

"Then said Daniel to Melzar,... Prove thy servants, I beseech thee, ten days; and let them give us pulse to eat, and water to drink....And in all matters of wisdom and understanding, that the king enquired of them, he found them <u>ten times better</u> than all the magicians and astrologers that were in all his realm." (vs. 11a-12,20)

Daniel knew what he was supposed to do in order to obey God. Although Daniel was no longer under the rules of his parents, he did not compromise in his beliefs. He was in a strange country with strange people, yet he chose to stand for what was right even when others were doing wrong. Young person, one day your parents, pastor, and youth pastor will be gone. You will be out on your own, and someone will challenge your beliefs. If you do not ground yourself in the Word of God, you will fall! Right now, begin deciding for yourself why you do what you do from the Bible. Prove God. Daniel asked for 10 days. After those 10 days God had brought them out as 10 times better than the heathen. This world may seem to have much to offer, but just as the 10 days prove, God has so much more to give to His children. Decide to do right. No matter who is around, where you are, and whatever the case. God will bless you for it and you will better because of it.

I Surrender All

Judson W. Van DeVenter
Winfield S. Weeden

1. All to Jesus I surrender, All to Him I freely give;
2. All to Jesus I surrender, Make me, Savior, wholly Thine;
3. All to Jesus I surrender, Lord, I give myself to Thee;

I will ever love and trust Him, In His presence daily live.
Let me feel Thy Holy Spirit, Truly know that Thou art mine.
Fill me with Thy love and power, Let Thy blessing fall on me.

I surrender all, I surrender all;
I surrender all, I surrender all;

All to Thee, my blessed Savior I surrender all.

I SURRENDER ALL

Judson Van DeVenter was born on a farm in Michigan in 1855. Following graduation from Hillsdale College, he became an art teacher and supervisor of art in the public schools of Sharon, Pennsylvania. He was, in addition, an accomplished musician, singer, and composer.

Van DeVenter was an active layman in his Methodist Episcopal Church. Recognizing his talent for the ministry, friends urged him to give up teaching and become an evangelist. Van DeVenter wavered for five years between becoming a recognized artist or devoting himself to ministry.

Finally, he surrendered his life to Christian service, and wrote the text of the hymn while conducting a meeting at the Ohio home of noted evangelist George Sebring. Following his decision to surrender his life to Christ, Van DeVenter traveled throughout the United States, England, and Scotland, doing evangelistic work.

Winfield S. Weeden, his associate and singer, assisted him for many years. Toward the end of his life, Van DeVenter moved to Florida, and was professor of hymnology at the Florida Bible Institute for four years in the 1920s. After his retirement, he remained involved in public speaking and religious gatherings. Van DeVenter published more than 60 hymns in his lifetime, but "I Surrender All" is his most famous. His tombstone is inscribed with the title of this hymn, "I Surrender All".

WEEK 13 — TEN x BETTER

Week (left top table)

SUN.		PSALM 85
MON.		PSALM 86
TUES.		PSALM 87
WED.		PSALM 88
THURS.		PSALM 89
FRI.		PSALM 90
SAT.		PSALM 91

(right top table)

SUN.	JOSH. 9-10	JOHN 17
MON.	JOSH. 11-12	JOHN 18
TUES.	JOSH. 13-14	JOHN 19
WED.	JOSH. 15-16	JOHN 20
THURS.	JOSH. 17-18	JOHN 21
FRI.	JOSH. 19-20	ACTS 1
SAT.	JOSH. 21-22	ACTS 2

TEN (bottom left)

SUN.	1 SAM. 17-19	EPH. 1-2
MON.	1 SAM. 20-22	EPH. 3-4
TUES.	1 SAM. 23-25	EPH. 5-6
WED.	1 SAM. 26-28	PHM. 1-2
THURS.	1 SAM. 29-31	PHM. 3-4
FRI.	2 SAM. 1-3	COL. 1-2
SAT.	2 SAM. 4-6	COL. 3-4

BETTER (bottom right)

SUN.	PSA. 27-32	JOHN 9-12
MON.	PSA. 33-38	JOHN 13-16
TUES.	PSA. 39-44	JOHN 17-20
WED.	PSA. 45-50	JOHN 21 - ACTS 3
THURS.	PSA. 51-56	ACTS 4-7
FRI.	PSA. 57-62	ACTS 8-11
SAT.	PSA. 63-68	ACTS 12-15

TEN THINGS BETTER

WEEK

SUN.	PSALM 92	JOSH. 23-24	ACTS 3
MON.	PSALM 93	JUDG. 1-2	ACTS 4
TUES.	PSALM 94	JUDG. 3-4	ACTS 5
WED.	PSALM 95	JUDG. 5-6	ACTS 6
THURS.	PSALM 96	JUDG. 7-8	ACTS 7
FRI.	PSALM 97	JUDG. 9-10	ACTS 8
SAT.	PSALM 98	JUDG. 11-12	ACTS 9

TEN × BETTER — 14 (TEN TIMES BETTER)

SUN.	2 SAM. 7-9	1 THES. 1-2	PSA. 69-74	ACTS 16-19
MON.	2 SAM. 10-12	1 THES. 3-4	PSA. 75-80	ACTS 20-23
TUES.	2 SAM. 13-15	1 THES. 5 - 2 THES. 1	PSA. 81-86	ACTS 24-27
WED.	2 SAM. 16-18	2 THES. 2-3	PSA. 87-92	ACTS 28 - ROM. 3
THURS.	2 SAM. 19-21	1 TIM. 1-2	PSA. 93-98	ROM. 4-7
FRI.	2 SAM. 22-24	1 TIM. 3-4	PSA. 99-104	ROM. 8-11
SAT.	1 KINGS 1-3	1 TIM. 5-6	PSA. 105-110	ROM. 12-15

TEN X BETTER

WEEK 15

SUN.	PSALM 99	SUN.	JUDG. 13-14	ACTS 10

SUN.	PSALM 99	1 KINGS 4-6	2 TIM. 1-2
MON.	PSALM 100	1 KINGS 7-9	2 TIM. 3-4
TUES.	PSALM 101	1 KINGS 10-12	TITUS 1-2
WED.	PSALM 102	1 KINGS 13-15	TITUS - PHM.
THURS.	PSALM 103	1 KINGS 16-18	HEB. 1-2
FRI.	PSALM 104	1 KINGS 19-21	HEB. 3-4
SAT.	PSALM 105	1 KGS. 22 - 2 KGS. 2	HEB. 5-6

Right Table

SUN.	JUDG. 13-14	PSA. 111-116	ACTS 10 / ROM. 16 - 1 COR. 3
MON.	JUDG. 15-16	PSA. 117-122	ACTS 11 / 1 COR. 4-7
TUES.	JUDG. 17-18	PSA. 123-128	ACTS 12 / 1 COR. 8-11
WED.	JUDG. 19-20	PSA. 129-134	ACTS 13 / 1 COR. 12-15
THURS.	JUDG. 21 - RUTH 1	PSA. 135-140	ACTS 14 / 1 COR. 16 - 2 COR. 3
FRI.	RUTH 2-3	PSA. 141-146	ACTS 15 / 2 COR. 4-7
SAT.	RUTH 4 - 1 SAM. 1	PSA. 147 - PROV. 2	ACTS 16 / 2 COR. 8-11

WEEK 16 — TEN X BETTER

SUN.		ACTS 17
MON.	1 SAM. 2-3	ACTS 18
TUES.	1 SAM. 4-5	ACTS 19
WED.	1 SAM. 6-7	ACTS 20
THURS.	1 SAM. 8-9	ACTS 21
FRI.	1 SAM. 10-11	ACTS 22
SAT.	1 SAM. 12-13	ACTS 23
	1 SAM. 14-15	

SUN.		PSALM 106
MON.		PSALM 107
TUES.		PSALM 108
WED.		PSALM 109
THURS.		PSALM 110
FRI.		PSALM 111
SAT.		PSALM 112

SUN.	2 KINGS 3-5	HEB. 7-8
MON.	2 KINGS 6-8	HEB. 9-10
TUES.	2 KINGS 9-11	HEB. 11-12
WED.	2 KINGS 12-14	HEB. 13 – JAS. 1
THURS.	2 KINGS 15-17	JAS. 2-3
FRI.	2 KINGS 18-20	JAS. 4-5
SAT.	2 KINGS 21-23	1 PET. 1-2

SUN.	PROV. 3-8	2 COR. 12 – GAL. 2
MON.	PROV. 9-14	GAL. 3-6
TUES.	PROV. 15-20	EPH. 1-4
WED.	PROV. 21-26	EPH. 5 – PHIL. 2
THURS.	PROV. 27 – ECC. 1	PHIL. 3 – COL. 2
FRI.	ECC. 2-7	COL. 3 – 1 THES. 2
SAT.	ECC. 8 – SONG. 1	1 THES. 3 – 2 THES. 1

✘ WAYS TO BE A BETTER YOU

1. SCHEDULE
2. EATING HABITS
3. WALK WITH GOD
4. ORGANIZATION
5. SPIRIT
6. REST
7. LAUGH/SMILE
8. BUDGET
9. EXERCISE
10. LOVE MORE

-William Davis

> **" NO MATTER WHAT A MAN'S PAST MAY HAVE BEEN, HIS FUTURE IS SPOTLESS.**
>
> — JOHN R. RICE

I'm on the Winning Side

HALE REEVES

I'm on the win-ning side. Well, I am
The win-ning side.

on the win-ning side, yes, I am on the win-ning side, Out in
I am on the win-ning side, I am on the win-ning side,

sin no more will I a-bide; I've en-
Out in sin no more will I a-bide, no more in sin a-bide;

list-ed in the fight for the cause of truth and right, Praise the
I've en-list-ed in the fight for the cause of truth and right,

Lord, I'm on the win - ning side!
Praise the Lord, I now am on the win-ning side.

I'M ON THE WINNING SIDE

Curtis Hutson was an Independent Fundamental Baptist pastor and editor of *The Sword of the Lord* (1980-1995). In 1961, Hutson heard Jack Hyles, Tom Malone, and John R. Rice preach at nearby Antioch Baptist Church. During that Sword of the Lord Conference, Hyles gave a two-hour soul-winning lecture. Hutson was convicted that he too should aggressively win the lost to Christ. The following Saturday, he led three people to the Lord. Every week thereafter for a number of years he led someone to Christ. He began to preach about soul winning, and his congregation began to follow his example.

In 1967, Hutson quit the post office to become a full-time pastor—at first for a salary of $75 a month. Between 1969 and 1972, the church grew from 350 to 2,300 members. In 1978, John R. Rice invited Hutson to become the associate editor of the fundamentalist newspaper The Sword of the Lord based in Murfreesboro, Tennessee. Two years later, Rice died and Hutson became editor. He served in this position for the remainder of his life while continuing to preach in churches across America. Weak, frail, and dying of cancer, Dr. Curtis Hutson sang "I'm on the winning side," at the Northside Baptist Church, in North Carolina. He preached a message entitled "Things that Are Different Are Not the Same" during the 1994 Southwide Baptist Fellowship. What an example we can see of having the grace and strength of God in the midst of all trials. In March of 1995 Curtis Hutson went to Heaven already "On the Winning Side"

-BACKSLIDER BEWARE-

1 SAMUEL 15:1-11

I have often heard Christians stand and testify and say "Praise God, I'm not wha[t] I used to be!" What a blessing it is to realize when Jesus saved us He exalted us from the pits of hell to the palaces of heaven, we went from lost to found, from broken to made whole, from sinners to saints! I'm glad when it comes to my sin, "I'm not what I used to be!"

Far too often I'm afraid some Christians could stand, testify and say the exact same thing, "I'm not what I used to be!" but rather than it being a positive statement, it could be a very negative indictment! "I used to be...a soul winner, separated, on fire for God" etc.

When a person is biblically born-again, they are instantly and eternally saved, sealed, and set for Heaven! BUT every child of God is more than able to fall away from the perfect will of God for their life! Every believer can backslide! Sins of varying types and sizes daily tempt you and I as Christians away from the blessings that God desires us to enjoy. They attempt to tow us BACK to bondage, emptiness, brokenness, and powerlessness!

Sir Isaac Newton once made a statement that is very significant not just for the science class but also for our spiritual life. He stated, *"To every action there is an equal and opposite reaction."* –There cannot be movement by one object, without it adversely, negatively, detrimentally affecting another object! It reminds me of the poem, *"My life will touch a thousand lives before the day is done, and leave a mark for bad or good ere sets the setting sun."*

Samuel loved Saul. He'd invested in him. When Saul did wrong it broke Samuel's heart. Verse 11 reads, "And it grieved Samuel..." Notice, it wasn't Samuel that sinned, it was not Samuel who messed up, it was not Samuel who backslide, but yet, at the very moment the Prophet received the news that Saul had sinned and slipped up, it was Samuel who was obviously, directly, deeply impacted Saul's disobedience! Let's strive to obey God. Let's stay in His will. Our lives ought to motivate others to be better Christians, not bitter or broken hearted.

-Justin Cooper

X VIRGINS

MATTHEW 25:1-13

"Then shall the kingdom of heaven be likened unto ten virgins, which took their lamps, and went forth to meet the bridegroom. And five of them were wise, and five were foolish. They that were foolish took their lamps, and took no oil with them: But the wise took oil in their vessels with their lamps. While the bridegroom tarried, they all slumbered and slept." (vs. 1-5)

In this parable there were 10 virgins preparing for the bridegroom to appear. Five were wise and five were foolish. The reason the five were considered foolish was for their lack of preparation. Young person, don't be like the foolish virgins and fail prepare for your life. As a teenager you should be preparing forwhat God has for you. He has a specific plan for your life, but it is up to you to prepare for that plan. Benjamin Franklin once said,*"If you fail to plan, you are planning to fail."* Some people say that a person will make the most important decisions of their life in their twenties and thirties, but I contend that a person will make the most important decisions of their life as a teenager. It is during those teenage years that one builds the foundation for their future. It is important that you are making the right decisions, and establishing Bible principles to live by. Young person I adjure you, prepare. Take time now to prepare for what God has for you in the future by daily walking with Him in prayer and Bible reading.

"To each there comes in their lifetime a special moment when they are figuratively tapped on the shoulder and offered the chance to do a very special thing, unique to them and fitted to their talents. What a tragedy if that moment finds them unprepared or unqualified for that which could have been their finest hour."
-Winston Churchill

WEEK 17 — TEN X BETTER

SUN.		PSALM 113			1 SAM. 16-17	ACTS 24
MON.		PSALM 114			1 SAM. 18-19	ACTS 25
TUES.		PSALM 115			1 SAM. 20-21	ACTS 26
WED.		PSALM 116			1 SAM. 22-23	ACTS 27
THURS.		PSALM 117			1 SAM. 24-25	ACTS 28
FRI.		PSALM 118			1 SAM. 26-27	ROM. 1
SAT.		PSALM 119			1 SAM. 28-29	ROM. 2
SUN.	2 KGS. 24 - 1 CHR. 1	1 PET. 3-4			SONG 2-8	2 THES. 2 - 1 TIM. 2
MON.	1 CHR. 2-4	1 PET. 5 - 2 PET. 1			ISA. 1-6	1 TIM. 3-6
TUES.	1 CHR. 5-7	2 PET. 2-3			ISA. 7-12	2 TIM. 1-4
WED.	1 CHR. 8-10	1 JOHN 1-2			ISA. 13-18	TITUS - PHM.
THURS.	1 CHR. 11-13	1 JOHN 3-4			ISA. 19-24	HEB. 1-4
FRI.	1 CHR. 14-16	1 JOHN. 5 - 2 JOHN			ISA. 25-30	HEB. 5-8
SAT.	1 CHR. 17-19	3 JOHN - JUDE			ISA. 31-36	HEB. 9-12

WEEK 18 — TEN X BETTER

SUN.	PSALM 120	1 SAM. 30-31
MON.	PROVERBS 1	2 SAM. 1-2
TUES.	PROVERBS 2	2 SAM. 3-4
WED.	PROVERBS 3	2 SAM. 5-6
THURS.	PROVERBS 4	2 SAM. 7-8
FRI.	PROVERBS 5	2 SAM. 9-10
SAT.	PROVERBS 6	2 SAM. 11-12

SUN.	1 CHR. 20-22	REV. 1-2
MON.	1 CHR. 23-25	REV. 3-4
TUES.	1 CHR. 26-28	REV. 5-6
WED.	1 CHR. 29 - 2 CHR. 2	REV. 7-8
THURS.	2 CHR. 3-5	REV. 9-10
FRI.	2 CHR. 6-8	REV. 11-12
SAT.	2 CHR. 9-11	REV. 13-14

SUN.	ISA. 37-42	ROM. 3
MON.	ISA. 43-48	ROM. 4
TUES.	ISA. 49-54	ROM. 5
WED.	ISA. 55-60	ROM. 6
THURS.	ISA. 61-66	ROM. 7
FRI.	JER. 1-6	ROM. 8
SAT.	JER. 7-12	ROM. 9

SUN.		HEB. 13 - JAS. 3
MON.		JAS. 4 - 1 PET. 2
TUES.		1 PET. 3 - 2 PET. 1
WED.		2 PET. 2 - 1 JOHN 2
THURS.		1 JHN. 3 - 2 JHN.
FRI.		3 JHN. - REV. 2
SAT.		REV. 3-6

WEEK 19 — TEN TIMES BETTER

SUN.		PROVERBS 7
MON.		PROVERBS 8
TUES.		PROVERBS 9
WED.		PROVERBS 10
THURS.		PROVERBS 11
FRI.		PROVERBS 12
SAT.		PROVERBS 13

SUN.	2 SAM. 13-14	ROM. 10
MON.	2 SAM. 15-16	ROM. 11
TUES.	2 SAM. 17-18	ROM. 12
WED.	2 SAM. 19-20	ROM. 13
THURS.	2 SAM. 21-22	ROM. 14
FRI.	2 SAM. 23-24	ROM. 15
SAT.	1 KINGS 1-2	ROM. 16

SUN.	2 CHR. 12-14	REV. 15-16
MON.	2 CHR. 15-17	REV. 17-18
TUES.	2 CHR. 18-20	REV. 19-20
WED.	2 CHR. 21-23	REV. 21-22
THURS.	2 CHR. 24-26	MATT. 1-2
FRI.	2 CHR. 27-29	MATT. 3-4
SAT.	2 CHR. 30-32	MATT. 5-6

SUN.	JER. 13-18	REV. 7-10
MON.	JER. 19-24	REV. 11-14
TUES.	JER. 25-30	REV. 15-18
WED.	JER. 31-36	REV. 19-22
THURS.	JER. 37-42	MATT. 1-4
FRI.	JER. 43-48	MATT. 5-8
SAT.	JER. 49 - LAM. 2	MATT. 9-12

WEEK 20

TEN X BETTER

SUN.	PROVERBS 14	SUN.	1 KINGS 3-4
MON.	PROVERBS 15	MON.	1 KINGS 5-6
TUES.	PROVERBS 16	TUES.	1 KINGS 7-8
WED.	PROVERBS 17	WED.	1 KINGS 9-10
THURS.	PROVERBS 18	THURS.	1 KINGS 11-12
FRI.	PROVERBS 19	FRI.	1 KINGS 13-14
SAT.	PROVERBS 20	SAT.	1 KINGS 15-16

SUN.	2 CHR. 33-35	SUN.	1 COR. 1
MON.	2 CHR. 36 - EZRA 2	MON.	1 COR. 2
TUES.	EZRA 3-5	TUES.	1 COR. 3
WED.	EZRA 6-8	WED.	1 COR. 4
THURS.	EZRA 9 - NEH. 1	THURS.	1 COR. 5
FRI.	NEH. 2-4	FRI.	1 COR. 6
SAT.	NEH. 5-7	SAT.	1 COR. 7

SUN.	MATT. 7-8	SUN.	LAM. 3 - EZEK. 3
MON.	MATT. 9-10	MON.	EZEK. 4-9
TUES.	MATT. 11-12	TUES.	EZEK. 10-15
WED.	MATT. 13-14	WED.	EZEK. 16-21
THURS.	MATT. 15-16	THURS.	EZEK. 22-27
FRI.	MATT. 17-18	FRI.	EZEK. 28-33
SAT.	MATT. 19-20	SAT.	EZEK. 34-39

		SUN.	MATT. 13-16
		MON.	MATT. 17-20
		TUES.	MATT. 21-24
		WED.	MATT. 25-28
		THURS.	MARK 1-4
		FRI.	MARK 5-8
		SAT.	MARK 9-12

✗ WAYS TO BE A BETTER INSTRUMENTALIST

1. STUDY AND LEARN FROM ADVANCED MUSICIANS TO ACQUIRE METHODS AND TECHNIQUES
2. FOLLOW THE SONG LEADER
3. PRACTICE UNTIL FULLY CONFIDENT IN THE SONG
4. ASK GOD TO MAKE YOUR MUSIC SPIRIT-FILLED
5. KEEP WORLDY INFLUENCES OUT OF YOUR MUSIC
6. KEEP THE EMPHASIS ON THE SONG AND NOT THE INSTURMENTALIST
7. KEEP THE MELODY PROMINENT
8. GET OTHERS INVOLVED
9. ENSURE YOUR INSTRUMENT IS TUNED WITH THE MAIN PIANO
10. WORK ON TIMING

-Jeremy Fugate

> **COURAGE ISN'T THE ABSENCE OF FEAR, BUT IS OBEDIENCE IN THE PRESENCE OF FEAR.**
>
> — PASTOR JEFF FUGATE

-THE BLOOD (PT. 1)-

HEBREWS 10:12 *"he had offered one sacrifice for sins for ever..."*

In the Old Testament, before Jesus Christ came in the flesh on earth to pay redemption's cost for all mankind once and for all; the Old Testament saints would offer up animals as an atonement or covering for their sin. The high priest would go into the holy of holies on behalf of the people and offered an atonement for the people's sin. This sacrificial atonement would happen once a year.

In Hebrews we see many comparisons of an Old and New Covenant. The old was set in the law, but the new much better. In Hebrews chapters 9 and 10, we see the words, "figure", "things to come", "pattern", and "shadow" referring back to the Old Testament; so all the burnt offerings and blood offerings that were made were just a picture of a much better sacrifice (Jesus Christ), the final sacrifice made for all sins and all mankind. The atonement for sin by an animal's blood in the Old Testament happened once a year, but the blood of Jesus Christ was a one and done payment for all mankind with no more payments required. How can one man pay the sin debt for all mankind?

In some foreign lands there are no price tags associated with merchandise, so a customer would take his merchandise to the front of the store where the owner of the store would be sitting. The customer would then lay his things on the counter and start placing money down beside it. Once enough money was placed down, the owner puts the money in the cash register and bags the items up, and the customer would know he had made enough payment for the items.

Over two thousand years ago, Christ left the portals of Heaven to come to earth. Jesus performed many miracles on earth, but Christ did not come to do miracles. Christ came to lay down his life on the cross of Calvary and pay sin's debt. Jesus died on Calvary and was placed in a borrowed tomb, but PRAISE GOD, three days later God raised HIM from the grave. When Christ arose from the grave, God was telling the entire world that He was satisfied with the payment that was made for sinful man.

-Chris Dallas

✗ SPIES

NUMBERS 13:4-16

"And the men, which Moses sent to search the land, who returned, and made all the congregation to murmur against him, by bringing up a slander upon the land, Even those men that did bring up the evil report upon the land, died by the plague before the LORD. But Joshua the son of Nun, and Caleb the son of Jephunneh, which were of the men that went to search the land, lived still." (Num. 14:36-38)

Do you know any of the other ten spies names? No, probably not. Most people do not know their names. The reason that no one knows their names is because they had no faith. Everyone, however, knows the names of Caleb and Joshua, because these two men had faith to step out and trust God. God had promised the land to Israel. He also promised to fight for them. Young person, is there a promise that God has made in His Word to you that you have been doubting? Don't be like the ten. Be a part of the two that trusted God.

BE BETTER, Have faith, JUST STEP OUT!

It Is Well with My Soul

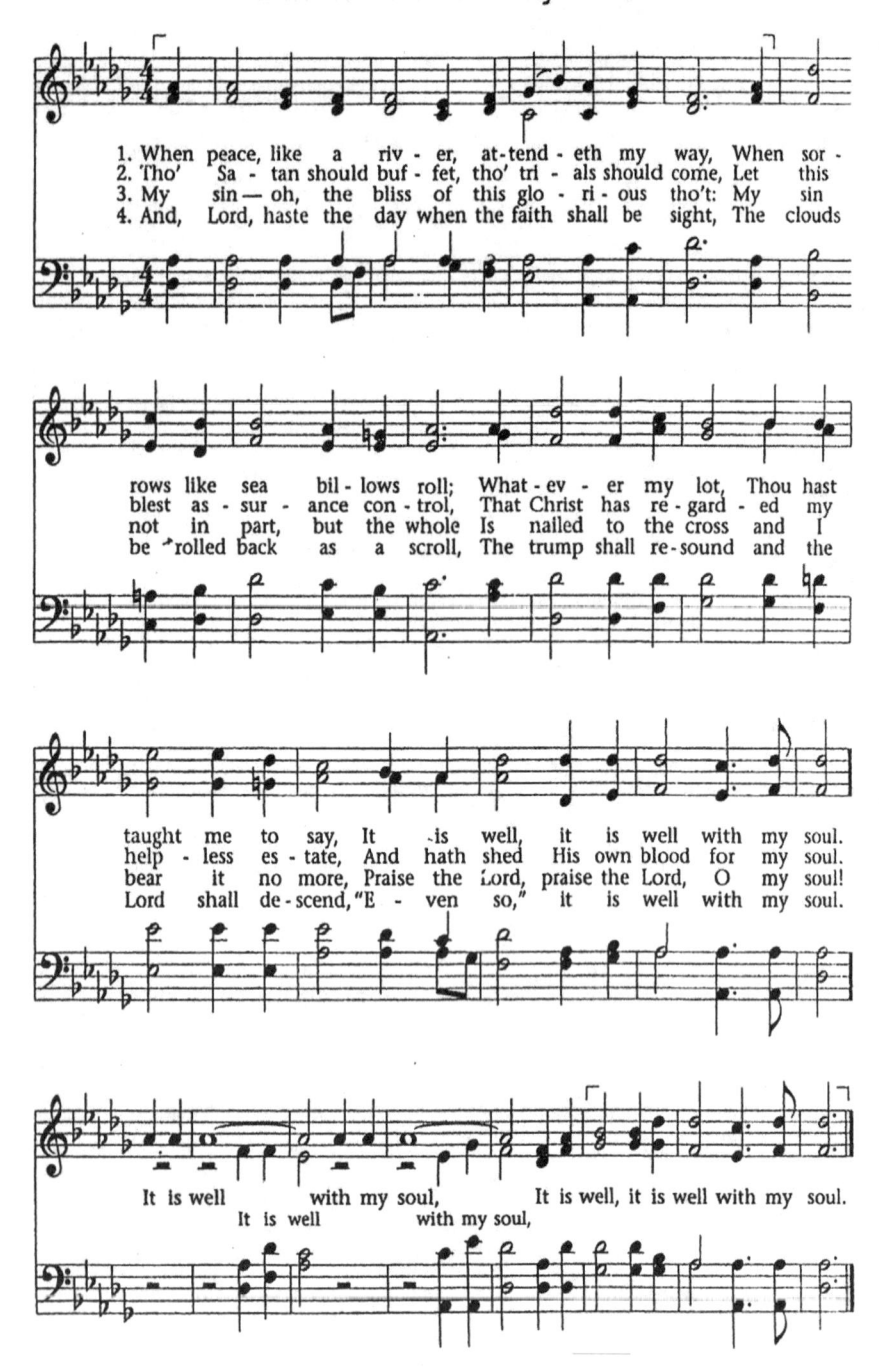

1. When peace, like a riv-er, at-tend-eth my way, When sor-rows like sea bil-lows roll; What-ev-er my lot, Thou hast taught me to say, It is well, it is well with my soul.
2. Tho' Sa-tan should buf-fet, tho' tri-als should come, Let this blest as-sur-ance con-trol, That Christ has re-gard-ed my help-less es-tate, And hath shed His own blood for my soul.
3. My sin — oh, the bliss of this glo-ri-ous tho't: My sin not in part, but the whole Is nailed to the cross and I bear it no more, Praise the Lord, praise the Lord, O my soul!
4. And, Lord, haste the day when the faith shall be sight, The clouds be rolled back as a scroll, The trump shall re-sound and the Lord shall de-scend, "E-ven so," it is well with my soul.

It is well with my soul, It is well, it is well with my soul.

IT IS WELL WITH MY SOUL

When the great Chicago fire consumed the Windy City in 1871, Horatio G. Spafford, an attorney heavily invested in real estate, lost a fortune. About that time, his only son, age 4, succumbed to scarlet fever. Horatio drowned his grief in work, pouring himself into rebuilding the city and assisting the 100,000 who had been left homeless.

In November of 1873, he decided to take his wife and daughters to Europe. Horatio was close to D. L. Moody and Ira Sankey, and desired to visit their evangelistic meetings in England, then enjoy a vacation.

When an urgent matter detained Horatio in New York, he decided to send his wife, Anna, and their four daughters, Maggie, Tanetta, Annie, and Bessie, on ahead. As he saw them settled into a cabin aboard ship unease filled his mind, and he moved them to a room closer to the bow of the ship. Then he said good-bye, promising to join them soon.

During the early hours of November 22, 1873, as the ship glided over smooth seas, the passengers were jolted from their bunks. The ship had collided with an iron sailing vessel, and water poured in like Niagara. The ship tilted dangerously. Screams, prayers, and oaths merged into a nightmare of unmeasured terror. Passengers clung to posts, tumbled through darkness, and were swept away by powerful currents of icy ocean. Loved ones fell from each other's grasp and disappeared into foaming blackness. Within two hours, the mighty ship vanished beneath the waters. The 226 fatalities included Maggie, Tanetta, Annie, and Bessie. Mrs. Spafford was found nearly unconscious, clinging to a piece of the wreckage. When the 47 survivors landed in Cardiff, Wales, she cabled her husband: "Saved Alone."

Horatio immediately booked passage to join his wife. In route, on a cold December night, the captain called him aside and said, "I believe we are now passing over the place where the ship went down." Spafford went to his cabin but found it hard to sleep. He said to himself, "It is well; the will of God be done." He then penned the words to his famous hymn, *"It Is Well With My Soul."*

WEEK 21 — TEN X BETTER

SUN.	PROVERBS 21
MON.	PROVERBS 22
TUES.	PROVERBS 23
WED.	PROVERBS 24
THURS.	PROVERBS 25
FRI.	PROVERBS 26
SAT.	PROVERBS 27

SUN.	1 KINGS 17-18	1 COR. 8
MON.	1 KINGS 19-20	1 COR. 9
TUES.	1 KINGS 21-22	1 COR. 10
WED.	2 KINGS 1-2	1 COR. 11
THURS.	2 KINGS 3-4	1 COR. 12
FRI.	2 KINGS 5-6	1 COR. 13
SAT.	2 KINGS 7-8	1 COR. 14

SUN.	NEH. 8-10	MATT. 21-22
MON.	NEH. 11-13	MATT. 23-24
TUES.	EST. 1-3	MATT. 25-26
WED.	EST. 4-6	MATT. 27-28
THURS.	EST. 7-9	MARK 1-2
FRI.	EST. 10 - JOB 2	MARK 3-4
SAT.	JOB 3-5	MARK 5-6

SUN.	EZEK. 40-45	MARK 13-16
MON.	EZEK. 46 - DAN. 3	LUKE 1-4
TUES.	DAN. 4-9	LUKE 5-8
WED.	DAN. 10 - JOEL 1	LUKE 9-12
THURS.	JOEL 2 - AM. 4	LUKE 13-16
FRI.	AMOS 5 - OB.	LUKE 17-20
SAT.	JON. - MIC. 2	LUKE 21-24

WEEK 22 — TEN TIMES BETTER

SUN.	PROVERBS 28	2 KINGS 9-10	1 COR. 15
MON.	PROVERBS 29	2 KINGS 11-12	1 COR. 16
TUES.	PROVERBS 30	2 KINGS 13-14	2 COR. 1
WED.	PROVERBS 31	2 KINGS 15-16	2 COR. 2
THURS.	PSALMS 121	2 KINGS 17-18	2 COR. 3
FRI.	PSALMS 122	2 KINGS 19-20	2 COR. 4
SAT.	PSALMS 123	2 KINGS 21-22	2 COR. 5

SUN.	JOB 6-8	MARK 7-8	MIC. 3 - NAH. 1	JOHN 1-4
MON.	JOB 9-11	MARK 9-10	NAH. 2 - ZEPH. 1	JOHN 5-8
TUES.	JOB 12-14	MARK 11-12	ZEPH. 2 - ZEC. 2	JOHN 9-12
WED.	JOB 15-17	MARK 13-14	ZEC. 3-8	JOHN 13-16
THURS.	JOB 18-20	MARK 15-16	ZEC. 9-14	JOHN 17-20
FRI.	JOB 21-23	LUKE 1-2	MAL. 1 - GEN. 2	JOHN 21 - ACTS 3
SAT.	JOB 24-26	LUKE 3-4	GEN. 3-8	ACTS 4-7

WEEK 23

TEN TIMES BETTER

SUN.		PSALMS 124	SUN.	2 KINGS 23-24	2 COR. 6
MON.		PSALMS 125	MON.	2 KGS. 25 - EZRA 1	2 COR. 7
TUES.		PSALMS 126	TUES.	EZRA 2-3	2 COR. 8
WED.		PSALMS 127	WED.	EZRA 4-5	2 COR. 9
THURS.		PSALMS 128	THURS.	EZRA 6-7	2 COR. 10
FRI.		PSALMS 129	FRI.	EZRA 8-9	2 COR. 11
SAT.		PSALMS 130	SAT.	EZRA 10 - NEH. 1	2 COR. 12

SUN.	JOB 6-8	MARK 7-8	SUN.	GEN. 9-14	ACTS 8-11
MON.	JOB 9-11	MARK 9-10	MON.	GEN. 15-20	ACTS 12-15
TUES.	JOB 12-14	MARK 11-12	TUES.	GEN. 21-26	ACTS 16-19
WED.	JOB 15-17	MARK 13-14	WED.	GEN. 27-32	ACTS 20-23
THURS.	JOB 18-20	MARK 15-16	THURS.	GEN. 33-38	ACTS 24-27
FRI.	JOB 21-23	LUKE 1-2	FRI.	GEN. 39-44	ACTS 28 - ROM. 3
SAT.	JOB 24-26	LUKE 3-4	SAT.	GEN. 45-50	ROM. 4-7

WEEK 24

TEN X BETTER

SUN.	PSALMS 131		NEH. 2-3	2 COR. 13
MON.	PSALMS 132		NEH. 4-5	GAL. 1
TUES.	PSALMS 133		NEH. 6-7	GAL. 2
WED.	PSALMS 134		NEH. 8-9	GAL. 3
THURS.	PSALMS 135		NEH. 10-11	GAL. 4
FRI.	PSALMS 136		NEH. 12-13	GAL. 5
SAT.	PSALMS 137		EST. 1-2	GAL. 6

SUN.	JOB 27-29	LUKE 5-6	EX. 1-6	ROM. 8-11
MON.	JOB 30-32	LUKE 7-8	EX. 7-12	ROM. 12-15
TUES.	JOB 33-35	LUKE 9-10	EX. 13-18	ROM. 16 - 1 COR. 3
WED.	JOB 36-38	LUKE 11-12	EX. 19-24	1 COR. 4-7
THURS.	JOB 39-41	LUKE 13-14	EX. 25-30	1 COR. 8-11
FRI.	JOB 42 - PSA. 2	LUKE 15-16	EX. 31-36	1 COR. 12-15
SAT.	PSA. 3-5	LUKE 17-18	EX. 37 - LEV. 2	1 COR. 16 - 2 COR. 3

✗ WAYS TO BE A BETTER STUDENT

1. **BE SPIRITUAL** - *Read your Bible and act on it*
2. **BE SPIRIT-FILLED** - *Nothing is more important*
3. **BE DILIGENT** - *You only get one chance at life*
4. **BE ORGANIZED** - *Messiness means more work for you later*
5. **BE PREPARED** - *Planning ahead takes time, but pays for itself many times over*
6. **BE FRIENDLY** - *Kind to everyone but olny yoked up with those going the right direction*
7. **BE APPROPRIATE** - *Always be above reproach*
8. **BE STUDIOUS** - *Study the "why" of things; get understanding*
9. **BE HUMBLE** - *Learn something from every person you can*
10. **BE HONEST** - *Your reputation is worth more than you think*

-James Tienhaara

> **SUCCESS IS ON THE SAME ROAD AS FAILURE; SUCCESS IS JUST A LITTLE FURTHER DOWN THE ROAD.**
>
> — JACK HYLES

-THE BLOOD (PT. 2)-

HEBREWS 10:12 *"...he had sacrifices of sins for ever..."*

In Part I of the devotional on "The Blood", we see the comparisons of the blood sacrifices of the Old Testament and the shed blood of the Lord Jesus Christ on the cross of Calvary and how the sacrifice of our Saviour was much better than that of animal. In this second part of the devotional on "The Blood", we will see the compliments of the blood and how we benefit from it.

First of all we need to understand that the lost man is under the condemnation a wrath of an almighty God, not because of any particular sin he committed but beca of the sin Adam committed in the garden when he broke God's commandment of partaking of the tree of the knowledge of good and evil. When Adam broke the commandment, there was a penalty of death added to his life, but that penalty not affected Adam, but all mankind from that day to this present day. (Read Romans 5: and Romans 6:23) And if a person died physically without knowing Christ spirituall that person would experience a second death apart from God in Hell for eternity. (Read Revelation 20:14-15) In the shed blood of animals in the Old Testament, man certainly to remain dead, deceived, doomed, and depraved because it was just a temporary atonement. The shedding of animal's blood could never completely tak man's sin away. (Read Hebrews 10: 3-4) But that's the bad news, Im glad to testify there's good news!! The Bible says in: Romans 5:8-9 "But God commendeth his lo toward us, in that, while we were yet sinners, Christ died for us. Much more then, b now justified by his blood, we shall be saved from wrath through him."

Let's see three blessings about the blood in Hebrews 10.

I. Free Gift of Salvation

There is nothing we can do to buy it or obtain it but it has already been paid for by shed blood on the cross.

Hebrews 10:12, *"But this man, after he had offered one sacrifice for sins for ever, s down on the right hand of God;"*

Romans 6:23, *"For the wages of sin is death; but the gift of God is eternal life throu Jesus Christ our Lord."*

-THE BLOOD (PT. 2)-

HEBREWS 10:12 *"...he had sacrifices of sins for ever..."*

> " I hear the Saviour say, thy strength indeed is small
> Child of weakness, watch and pray,
> find in me thine all in all
> Jesus paid it all, All to him I owe
> sin had left a crimson stain,
> he washed it white as snow"

II. Forgiveness of Sins

One thing that everyone of us stand in need of is this thing called forgiveness, but we serve a God that not only forgives but forgets our sin never to be remembered.

Hebrews 10:17- *"And their sins and iniquities will I remember no more."*

Psalm 103:12- *"As far as the east is from the west, so far hath he removed our transgressions from us."*

I John 1:9- *"If we confess our sins, he is faithful and just to forgive us our sins, and to cleanse us from all unrighteousness."*

III. Forever Secure

The Bible gives us the promise if we put our faith and trust in the shed blood for salvation, that we will escape Hell's flame and go to Heaven one day and there is not a sin we can commit from that day forward that can or will ever take our salvation away.

Hebrews 10:10- *"By the which will we are sanctified through the offering of the body of Jesus Christ once for all."*

John 10:28- *"And I give unto them eternal life; and they shall never perish, neither shall any man pluck them out of my hand."*

> "What can wash away my sin?
> Nothing but the blood of Jesus
> What can make me whole agai?
> Nothing but the blood of Jesus

-Chris Dallas

Living for Jesus

1. Liv-ing for Je-sus, a life that is true, Striv-ing to please Him in all that I do; Yield-ing al-le-giance, glad-heart-ed and free, This is the path-way of bless-ing for me.

2. Liv-ing for Je-sus Who died in my place, Bear-ing on Cal-v'ry my sin and dis-grace; Such love con-strains me to an-swer His call, Fol-low His lead-ing and give Him my all.

3. Liv-ing for Je-sus, wher-ev-er I am, Do-ing each du-ty in His ho-ly Name; Will-ing to suf-fer af-flic-tion and loss, Deem-ing each tri-al a part of my cross.

4. Liv-ing for Je-sus through earth's lit-tle while, My dear-est treas-ure, the light of His smile; Seek-ing the lost ones He died to re-deem, Bring-ing the wear-y to find rest in Him.

Refrain (slower)

O Je-sus, Lord and Sav-ior, I give my-self to Thee, For Thou, in Thy a-tone-ment, didst give Thy-self for me; I own no oth-er Mas-ter, my heart shall be Thy throne; My life I give, hence-forth to live, O Christ, for Thee a-lone.

LIVING FOR JESUS

A native of a small Kentucky town, Thomas Obadiah Chisholm lacked formal education. Nevertheless, he became a teacher at age 16 and associate editor of his hometown weekly newspaper at age 21. In 1893 Chisholm became a Christian through the ministry of Henry Clay Morrison, the founder of Asbury College. Though health would keep Chisholm from serving in the ministry full time, Chisholm served briefly as a pastor in 1903 in Scottsville, KY.

C. Harold Lowden composed the tune for "Living for Jesus" in 1915, and first published the song under the title 'Sunshine Song'. Early in 1917, while preparing a collection of hymns for publication, he came across this song and was convinced that the tune needed a stronger text. He substituted 'Living for Jesus' for the original title and sent the tune to Thomas O. Chisholm for a new text.

Even though Chisholm, an accomplished poet, protested that he had never written a text for a pre-existing tune, Lowden insisted, telling the author that he believed God had led him to select Chisholm to provide a text for this music. Within a short time, Chisholm returned the tune with four stanzas and a refrain.

As in most gospel songs, the theme may be found in the refrain. The refrain stresses personal commitment to Jesus Christ because of what he did for us through his atonement. This is total commitment as the singer states, "I own no other master" than Christ, who sits on the "throne" of our heart.

Our mission is to bring the lost ones to Christ and, in doing so, submitting totally to Him. The biblical basis for this song may be found in the famous passage, Romans 12:1a, beginning with "I beseech you therefore, brethren, by the mercies of God that ye present your bodies a living sacrifice. . . ." Chisholm once stated his purpose for writing songs: "I have sought to be true to the Word, and to avoid flippant and catchy titles and treatment. I have greatly desired that each hymn or people might have some definite message to the hearts for whom it was written." During his life, Chisholm would be responsible for composing over 1,200 poems.

WEEK 25 — TEN X BETTER

SUN.	PSALMS 138	SUN.	EST. 3-4
MON.	PSALMS 139	MON.	EST. 5-6
TUES.	PSALMS 140	TUES.	EST. 7-8
WED.	PSALMS 141	WED.	EST. 9-10
THURS.	PSALMS 142	THURS.	JOB. 1-2
FRI.	PSALMS 143	FRI.	JOB 3-4
SAT.	PSALMS 144	SAT.	JOB 5-6

SUN.	LUKE 19-20	SUN.	EPH. 1
MON.	LUKE 21-22	MON.	EPH. 2
TUES.	LUKE 23-24	TUES.	EPH. 3
WED.	JOHN 1-2	WED.	EPH. 4
THURS.	JOHN 3-4	THURS.	EPH. 5
FRI.	JOHN 5-6	FRI.	EPH. 6
SAT.	JOHN 7-8	SAT.	PHIL. 1

SUN.	PSA. 6-8	SUN.	2 COR. 4-7
MON.	PSA. 9-11	MON.	2 COR. 8-11
TUES.	PSA. 12-14	TUES.	2 COR. 12 - GAL. 2
WED.	PSA. 15-17	WED.	GAL. 3 - 6
THURS.	PSA. 18-20	THURS.	LEV. 27 - NUM. 5 / EPH. 1-4
FRI.	PSA. 21-23	FRI.	NUM. 6-11 / EPH. 5 - PHIL. 2
SAT.	PSA. 24-26	SAT.	NUM. 12-17 / PHIL. 3 - COL. 2

SUN.	LEV. 3-8
MON.	LEV. 9-14
TUES.	LEV. 15-20
WED.	LEV. 21-26

TEN TIMES BETTER

WEEK 26 — TEN TIMES BETTER

SUN.	PSALMS 145	JOB 7-8	PHIL. 2
MON.	PSALMS 146	JOB 9-10	PHIL. 3
TUES.	PSALMS 147	JOB 11-12	PHIL. 4
WED.	PSALMS 148	JOB 13-14	COL. 1
THURS.	PSALMS 149	JOB 15-16	COL. 2
FRI.	PSALMS 150	JOB 17-18	COL. 3
SAT.	PSALMS 1	JOB 19-20	COL. 4

SUN.	PSA. 27-29	JOHN 9-10	NUM. 18-23	COL. 3 - 1 THES. 2
MON.	PSA. 30-32	JOHN 11-12	NUM. 24-29	1 THES. 3 - 2 THES. 1
TUES.	PSA. 33-35	JOHN 13-14	NUM. 30-35	2 THES. 2 - 1 TIM. 2
WED.	PSA. 36-38	JOHN 15-16	NUM. 36 - DEUT. 5	1 TIM. 3-6
THURS.	PSA. 39-41	JOHN 17-18	DEUT. 6-11	2 TIM. 1-4
FRI.	PSA. 42-44	JOHN 19-20	DEUT. 12-17	TITUS - PHM.
SAT.	PSA. 45-47	JOHN 21 - ACTS 1	DEUT. 18-23	HEB. 1-4

WEEK 27 — TEN X BETTER

SUN.		PSALMS 2	SUN.	JOB 21-22	1 THES. 1		
MON.		PSALMS 3	MON.	JOB 23-24	1 THES. 2		
TUES.		PSALMS 4	TUES.	JOB 25-26	1 THES. 3		
WED.		PSALMS 5	WED.	JOB 27-28	1 THES. 4		
THURS.		PSALMS 6	THURS.	JOB 29-30	1 THES. 5		
FRI.		PSALMS 7	FRI.	JOB 31-32	2 THES. 1		
SAT.		PSALMS 8	SAT.	JOB 33-34	2 THES. 2		

Day	TEN		Day		BETTER
SUN.	PSA. 48-50	ACTS 2-3	SUN.	DEUT. 24-29	HEB. 5-8
MON.	PSA. 51-53	ACTS 4-5	MON.	DEUT. 30 - JOSH. 1	HEB. 9-12
TUES.	PSA. 54-56	ACTS 6-7	TUES.	JOSH. 2-7	HEB. 13 - JAM. 3
WED.	PSA. 57-59	ACTS 8-9	WED.	JOSH. 8-13	JAS. 4 - 1 PET. 2
THURS.	PSA. 60-62	ACTS 10-11	THURS.	JOSH. 14-19	1 PET. 3 - 2 PET. 1
FRI.	PSA. 63-65	ACTS 12-13	FRI.	JOSH. 20 - JUDG. 1	2 PET. 2 - 1 JHN. 2
SAT.	PSA. 66-68	ACTS 14-15	SAT.	JUDG. 2-7	1 JHN. 3 - 2 JHN.

TEN TIMES BETTER

TEN X BETTER

WEEK 28

SUN.	PSALMS 9	
MON.	PSALMS 10	
TUES.	PSALMS 11	
WED.	PSALMS 12	
THURS.	PSALMS 13	
FRI.	PSALMS 14	
SAT.	PSALMS 15	

SUN.	JOB 35-36	2 THES. 3
MON.	JOB 37-38	1 TIM. 1
TUES.	JOB 39-40	1 TIM. 2
WED.	JOB 41-42	1 TIM. 3
THURS.	PSA. 1-2	1 TIM. 4
FRI.	PSA. 3-4	1 TIM. 5
SAT.	PSA. 5-6	1 TIM. 6

SUN.	PSA. 69-71	ACTS 16-17
MON.	PSA. 72-74	ACTS 18-19
TUES.	PSA. 75-77	ACTS 20-21
WED.	PSA. 78-80	ACTS 22-23
THURS.	PSA. 81-83	ACTS 24-25
FRI.	PSA. 84-86	ACTS 26-27
SAT.	PSA. 87-89	ACTS 28 - ROM. 1

SUN.	JUDG. 8-13	3 JHN. - REV. 2
MON.	JUDG. 14-19	REV. 3-6
TUES.	JUDG. 20 - RUTH	REV. 7-10
WED.	1 SAM. 1-6	REV. 11-14
THURS.	1 SAM. 7-12	REV. 15-18
FRI.	1 SAM. 13-18	REV. 19-22
SAT.	1 SAM. 19-24	MATT. 1-4

X WAYS TO BE A BETTER CHRISTIAN

1. **READ THE BIBLE**
2. **PRAY**
3. **GO TO CHURCH**
4. **MAKE GOOD FRIENDS**
5. **TITHE**
6. **SURRENDER**
7. **SEPARATE FROM THE WORLD**
8. **WITNESS**
9. **SING GOOD SONGS**
10. **SERVE OTHERS**

-William Davis

> **BY PERSEVERANCE THE SNAIL REACHED THE ARK.**
>
> — CHARLES SPURGEON

Never Give Up

FANNY J. CROSBY
I. ALLEN SANKEY

Nev - er give up, Nev - er give up,
Nev-er give up, nev-er give up, Nev-er give up, nev-er give up,

Nev - er give up to thy sor-rows, Je-sus will bid them de-part;

Trust in the Lord, Trust in the Lord,
Trust in the Lord, trust in the Lord, Trust in the Lord, trust in the Lord,

Sing when your tri-als are great-est, Trust in the Lord and take heart.

NEVER GIVE UP

Frances Jane Crosby was born in Putnam County, NY., March 24, 1820. She became blind at the age of six weeks from maltreatment to her eyes during a spell of sickness. At the age of fifteen she entered the New York Institution for the Blind, where she received a good education. She became a teacher in the institution in 1847 and continued her work until March 1, 1858. She taught English grammar, rhetoric and American history. While teaching at the institution she met Presidents Van Buren and Tyler, Senator Henry Clay, Governor W. H. Seward, General Winfield Scott, and other distinguished characters of American history.

Concerning Henry Clay, she gives the following: "When Mr. Clay came to the institution during his last visit to New York, I was selected to welcome him with a poem. Six months before he had lost a son at the battle of Monterey, and I had sent him some verses. In my address I carefully avoided any allusion to them, in order not to wound him. When I had finished, he drew my arm in his, and, addressing the audience, said through his tears: 'This is not the first poem for which I am indebted to this lady. Six months ago, she sent me some lines on the death of my dear son.' Both of us were overcome for a few moments. Soon, by a splendid effort, Mr. Clay recovered himself, but I could not control my tears." Miss Fanny Crosby had the honor of being the first woman whose voice was heard publicly in the Senate Chamber at Washington. In addition to the thousands of hymns that she has written, many of which have not been set to music, she has published four volumes of verses. Though these show the poetical bent of her mind, they have little to do with her world-wide fame. It is as a writer of Sunday-school songs and gospel hymns that she is known wherever the English language is spoken, and, in fact, wherever any other language is heard.

In the hymn, "Never Give Up," she tells of how we should never allow our sadness and sorrows to overtake us. We must trust in the Lord and "Sing when your trials are greatest." This continued to be her philosophy, "Never Give Up!" She says that had it not been for her affliction she might not have so good an education, nor so great an influence, and certainly not so fine a memory. She knew a great many portions of the Bible by heart and had committed to memory the first four books of the Old Testament, and also the four Gospels before she was ten years of age.

X LEPERS

LUKE 17:11-19

"And one of them, when he saw that he was healed, turned back, and with a loud voice glorified God, And fell down on his face at his feet, giving him thanks: and he was a Samaritan. And Jesus answering said, Were there not ten cleansed? but where are the nine? There are not found that returned to give glory to God, save this stranger. And he said unto him, Arise, go thy way: thy faith hath made thee whole." (vs. 15-19)

10 lepers came to Jesus needing a miracle. While nine lepers were healed from their leprosy, only the one that went back to Jesus and gave Him thanks was made whole. Young person, the attitude of gratitude is lacking in our generation. In 2 Timothy 3:2 we find Paul warning Timothy of this sin and spirit of unthankfulness being prevalent in the last days. We have so much to thank Him for. So, let us BE BETTER by being THANKFUL!

-SERVE GOD-

PROVERBS 10:22, *"The blessing of the LORD, it maketh rich, and he added no sorrow with it."*

True blessing, joy, peace and fulfillment come from God. They come from Him as we seek and follow His plan for our lives. All of us should volunteer to serve God. In some cases this means we will be in "full-time ministry" and receive our income from the ministry. In other cases, we may receive income from a "secular" job, but we should still be "full-time" servants of God. The following are eight reasons that YOU and I should volunteer to serve God with your life.

1. You and I are bought with a price by God. We don't belong to ourselves, God owns us. I Corinthians 6:19,20.

2. You and I owe God a debt. He died for us, the least you and I can do is live for Him. Revelation 5:9; I Peter 1:18,19

3. You and I love God. John 14:15,21

4. People need to be saved. If someone does not hear the Gospel, he cannot trust Christ. People who die without being saved will be in hell forever. Romans 10:14; Romans 1:14.

5. You and I owe it to people who have invested in us. Our parents, pastors, youth pastors, bus captains, teachers and more. II Timothy 2:2.

6. America needs to be saved. And God will spare our country if there are enough righteous here. You and I can make a difference. Genesis 18:32

7. You and I will receive eternal rewards for whatever we do for Christ. Matthew 6:19,20

8. Serving God brings joy in this life! God will bless you as you serve Him. He gives a life that brings joy here, and will bring joy in heaven. John 10:10; John 15:9-11.

-Jim Jorgenson

✗ WAYS TO HAVE AN ✗-CELLENT SPIRIT

1. KEEP A "THANK YOU" FOLDER/JOURNAL.
2. REPLACE "HAVE TO" WITH "GET TO".
3. FOLLOW AUTHORITY.
4. ESCAPE NEGATIVITY AND CRITICISM.
5. CARRY "HAPPY" WITH YOU.
6. CELEBRATE THE SMALL THINGS.
7. BE A GIVER NOT A TAKER.
8. FORGIVE. DON'T BE BITTER.
9. MAKE SOMEONE ELSE SMILE.
10. SING GODLY MUSIC.

-William Davis

✘ THINGS MONEY CAN'T BUY

1. **CHARACTER**
2. **CLASS**
3. **COMMON SENSE**
4. **INTEGRITY**
5. **LOVE**
6. **MANNERS**
7. **MORALS**
8. **PATIENCE**
9. **RESPECT**
10. **TRUST**

-William Davis

WEEK 29

TEN

SUN.	PSALMS 16	SUN.	PSA. 7-8
MON.	PSALMS 17	MON.	PSA. 9-10
TUES.	PSALMS 18	TUES.	PSA. 11-12
WED.	PSALMS 19	WED.	PSA. 13-14
THURS.	PSALMS 20	THURS.	PSA. 15-16
FRI.	PSALMS 21	FRI.	PSA. 17-18
SAT.	PSALMS 22	SAT.	PSA. 19-20

BETTER

SUN.	PSA. 90-92	ROM. 2-3	SUN.	1 SAM. 25-30	MATT. 5-8
MON.	PSA. 93-95	ROM. 4-5	MON.	1 SAM. 31 - 2 SAM. 5	MATT. 9-12
TUES.	PSA. 96-98	ROM. 6-7	TUES.	2 SAM. 6-11	MATT. 13-16
WED.	PSA. 99-101	ROM. 8-9	WED.	2 SAM. 12-17	MATT. 17-20
THURS.	PSA. 102-104	ROM. 10-11	THURS.	2 SAM. 18-23	MATT. 21-24
FRI.	PSA. 105-107	ROM. 12-13	FRI.	2 SAM. 24 - 1 KGS. 5	MATT. 25-28
SAT.	PSA. 108-110	ROM. 14-15	SAT.	1 KINGS. 6-11	MARK 1-4

TEN TIMES BETTER

TEN X BETTER

WEEK 30

SUN.	PSALMS 23
MON.	PSALMS 24
TUES.	PSALMS 25
WED.	PSALMS 26
THURS.	PSALMS 27
FRI.	PSALMS 28
SAT.	PSALMS 29

SUN.		PHILEMON
MON.	PSA. 21-22	HEB. 1
TUES.	PSA. 23-24	HEB. 2
WED.	PSA. 25-26	HEB. 3
THURS.	PSA. 27-28	HEB. 4
FRI.	PSA. 29-30	HEB. 5
SAT.	PSA. 31-32	HEB. 6
	PSA. 33-34	

SUN.	PSA. 111-113	ROM. 16 - 1 COR. 1
MON.	PSA. 114-116	1 COR. 2-3
TUES.	PSA. 117-119	1 COR. 4-5
WED.	PSA. 120-122	1 COR. 6-7
THURS.	PSA. 123-125	1 COR. 8-9
FRI.	PSA. 126-128	1 COR. 10-11
SAT.	PSA. 129-131	1 COR. 12-13

SUN.	1 KINGS 12-17	MARK 5-8
MON.	1 KINGS 18 - 2 KINGS 1	MARK 9-12
TUES.	2 KINGS 2-7	MARK 13-16
WED.	2 KINGS 8-13	LUKE 1-4
THURS.	2 KINGS 14-19	LUKE 5-8
FRI.	2 KINGS 20-25	LUKE 9-12
SAT.	1 CHR. 1-6	LUKE 13-16

WEEK 31 — TEN TIMES BETTER

SUN.	PSALMS 30	1 COR. 14-15	SUN.	PSA. 35-36	HEB. 7
MON.	PSALMS 31	1 COR. 16 - 2 COR. 1	MON.	PSA. 37-38	HEB. 8
TUES.	PSALMS 32	2 COR. 2-3	TUES.	PSA. 39-40	HEB. 9
WED.	PSALMS 33	2 COR. 4-5	WED.	PSA. 41-42	HEB. 10
THURS.	PSALMS 34	2 COR. 6-7	THURS.	PSA. 43-44	HEB. 11
FRI.	PSALMS 35	2 COR. 8-9	FRI.	PSA. 45-46	HEB. 12
SAT.	PSALMS 36	2 COR. 10-11	SAT.	PSA. 47-48	HEB. 13

SUN.	PSA. 132-134		SUN.	1 CHR. 7-12	LUKE 17-20
MON.	PSA. 135-137		MON.	1 CHR. 13-18	LUKE 21-24
TUES.	PSA. 138-140		TUES.	1 CHR. 19-24	JOHN 1-4
WED.	PSA. 141-143		WED.	1 CHR. 25 - 2 CHR. 1	JOHN 5-8
THURS.	PSA. 144-146		THURS.	2 CHR. 2-7	JOHN 9-12
FRI.	PSA. 145-148		FRI.	2 CHR. 8-13	JOHN 13-16
SAT.	PSA. 149 - PROV. 1		SAT.	2 CHR. 14-19	JOHN 17-20

WEEK 32 — TEN X BETTER

SUN.	PSALMS 37
MON.	PSALMS 38
TUES.	PSALMS 39
WED.	PSALMS 40
THURS.	PSALMS 41
FRI.	PSALMS 42
SAT.	PSALMS 43

SUN.	PSA. 49-50
MON.	PSA. 51-52
TUES.	PSA. 53-54
WED.	PSA. 55-56
THURS.	PSA. 57-58
FRI.	PSA. 59-60
SAT.	PSA. 61-62

SUN.	JAMES 1
MON.	JAMES 2
TUES.	JAMES 3
WED.	JAMES 4
THURS.	JAMES 5
FRI.	1 PET. 1
SAT.	1 PET. 2

SUN.	PROV. 2-4
MON.	PROV. 5-7
TUES.	PROV. 8-10
WED.	PROV. 11-13
THURS.	PROV. 14-16
FRI.	PROV. 17-19
SAT.	PROV. 20-22

SUN.	2 COR. 12-13
MON.	GAL. 1-2
TUES.	GAL. 3-4
WED.	GAL. 5-6
THURS.	EPH. 1-2
FRI.	EPH. 3-4
SAT.	EPH. 5-6

SUN.	2 CHR. 20-25
MON.	2 CHR. 26-31
TUES.	2 CHR. 32 - EZRA 1
WED.	EZRA 2-7
THURS.	EZRA 8 - NEH. 3
FRI.	NEH. 4-9
SAT.	NEH. 10 - EST. 2

SUN.	JOHN 21 - ACTS 3
MON.	ACTS 4-7
TUES.	ACTS 8-11
WED.	ACTS 12-15
THURS.	ACTS 16-19
FRI.	ACTS 20-23
SAT.	ACTS 24-27

X WAYS TO BE A BETTER FRIEND

1. **LISTEN**
2. **PRAY**
3. **LOVE**
4. **HELP**
5. **FORGIVE**
6. **FELLOWSHIP**
7. **GIVE**
8. **COMMUNICATE**
9. **BE HONEST**
10. **SUPPORT**

-William Davis

> **TO MAKE A DIFFERENCE, YOU HAVE TO BE DIFFERENT.**
>
> — **WILLIAM DAVIS**

KEY CHAPTERS IN THE O.T.

1. **GENESIS 1** - *The Creation*
2. **EXODUS 20** - *The Law*
3. **1 SAMUEL 17** - *The Defeat of Goliath*
4. **2 CHRONICLES 34** - *The Revival Under Josiah*
5. **PSALMS 23** - *The Shepherd Psalm*
6. **PSALMS 51** - *The Psalm of Confession*
7. **PROVERBS 1** - *The Instruction of Wisdom*
8. **PROVERBS 31** - *The Virtuous Woman*
9. **ISAIAH 6** - *The Throne of God*
10. **ISAIAH 53** - *The Messiah*

✘ KEY CHAPTERS IN THE N.T.

1. **MATTHEW 5-7** - *The Sermon on the Mount*
2. **LUKE 2** - *The Birth of Christ*
3. **JOHN 3** - *The New Birth*
4. **ROMANS 6-8** - *The Spiritual Life*
5. **1 CORINTHIANS 13** - *Christian Love*
6. **EPHESIANS 6** - *Spiritual Warfare*
7. **1 THESSALONIANS 4** - *The Second Coming of the Lord*
8. **HEBREWS 11** - *The Hall of Faith*
9. **JAMES 3** - *The Tongue*
10. **1 JOHN 1** - *The Fellowship of the Christian*

NOTHING BETWEEN

1. Nothing between my soul and my Savior, Naught of this world's delusive dream; I have renounced all sinful pleasure;
2. Nothing between like worldly pleasure; Habits of life, tho' harmless they seem, Must not my heart from Him ever sever;
3. Nothing between like pride or station; Self or friends shall not intervene; Tho' it may cost me much tribulation,
4. Nothing between, e'en many hard trials, Tho' the whole world against me convene; Watching with pray'r and much self denial, I'll

D.S.—The least of his favor,

Fine Chorus

Jesus is mine,
He is my all,
I am resolved, there's nothing between. Nothing between my soul and the
triumph at last,
Keep the way clear! Let nothing between.

D.S. al Fine

Savior, So that His blessed face my be seen; Nothing preventing

NOTHING BETWEEN

Charles Tindley was born into slavery in 1851. Charles wrote, "My father was poor as it relates to this world's goods, but was rich in the grace of God. He was unable to send me to school or to keep me with him at his little home. It therefore became my lot to be hired out... The people with whom I lived were not all good. Some of them were very cruel... I used to find bits of newspaper on the roadside... in order to study the A,B,C,'s from them. During the day I would gather pine knots, and when the people were asleep at night I would light these pine knots, and ... with fire-coals, mark all the words I could make out. I continued in this way, and without any teacher, until I could read the Bible." One day Charles slipped into church and sat in the back. When the preacher asked any child who could read the Bible to come forward, Charles went to the front. He later recalled the odd looks people gave him and overheard someone refer to him as "the boy with the bare feet." From that moment, Charles resolved to gain an education.

Later he would move to Philadelphia, and would there give his life to Christ. His entrance into "full-time" ministry began humbly – as the church janitor. "My first plan was to buy every book I could," he explained. "Then I entered by correspondence all the schools to which my limited means would afford ... Thus while I was unable to go through the schools, I was able to let the schools go through me." In 1885, he applied for ordination. One of the other candidates asked him, "How do you expect to pass your examination? The other candidates and I have diplomas. What do you hold?" "Nothing but a broom," was Tindley's reply. But the boy with the broom went on to become a world-famous pastor, preacher, and hymnist. One evening as he studied, according to most accounts of the story, a piece of paper, caught by the wind, flew across Charles' lamp, causing a shadow to fall over his writing. Pausing, Charles considered the power of a sin to darken his soul, and out of that came his great hymn: *"Nothing Between."*

WEEK 33

TEN

SUN.	PSALMS 44	PHIL. 1-2
MON.	PSALMS 45	PHIL. 3-4
TUES.	PSALMS 46	COL. 1-2
WED.	PSALMS 47	COL. 3-4
THURS.	PSALMS 48	1 THES. 1-2
FRI.	PSALMS 49	1 THES. 3-4
SAT.	PSALMS 50	1 THES. 5 - 2 THES. 1

SUN.	PSA. 63-64	1 PET. 3
MON.	PSA. 65-66	1 PET. 4
TUES.	PSA. 67-68	1 PET. 5
WED.	PSA. 69-70	2 PET. 1
THURS.	PSA. 71-72	2 PET. 2
FRI.	PSA. 73-74	2 PET. 3
SAT.	PSA. 75-76	1 JHN. 1

BETTER

SUN.	PROV. 23-25	EST. 3-8
MON.	PROV. 26-28	EST. 9 - JOB 4
TUES.	PROV. 29-31	JOB 5-10
WED.	ECC. 1-3	JOB 11-16
THURS.	ECC. 4-6	JOB 17-22
FRI.	ECC. 7-9	JOB 23-28
SAT.	ECC. 10-12	JOB 29-34

SUN.		ACTS 28 - ROM. 3
MON.		ROM. 4-7
TUES.		ROM. 8-11
WED.		ROM. 12-15
THURS.		ROM. 16 - 1 COR. 3
FRI.		1 COR. 4-7
SAT.		1 COR. 8-11

TEN TIMES BETTER

WEEK 34 — TEN TIMES BETTER

SUN.	PSALMS 51	SUN.	PSA. 77-78	1 JHN. 2
MON.	PSALMS 52	MON.	PSA. 79-80	1 JHN. 3
TUES.	PSALMS 53	TUES.	PSA. 81-82	1 JHN. 4
WED.	PSALMS 54	WED.	PSA. 83-84	1 JHN. 5
THURS.	PSALMS 55	THURS.	PSA. 85-86	2 JOHN
FRI.	PSALMS 56	FRI.	PSA. 87-88	3 JOHN
SAT.	PSALMS 57	SAT.	PSA. 89-90	JUDE

Day	Isaiah/Song	Timothy/Titus	Day	Job/Psalms	Corinthians/Galatians/Ephesians
SUN.	SONG. 1-3	2 THES. 2-3	SUN.	JOB 35-40	1 COR. 12-15
MON.	SONG. 4-6	1 TIM. 1-2	MON.	JOB 41 - PSA. 4	1 COR. 16 - 2 COR. 3
TUES.	SONG. 7 - ISA. 1	1 TIM. 3-4	TUES.	PSA. 5-10	2 COR. 4-7
WED.	ISA. 2-4	1 TIM. 5-6	WED.	PSA. 11-16	2 COR. 8-11
THURS.	ISA. 5-7	2 TIM. 1-2	THURS.	PSA. 17-22	2 COR. 12 - GAL. 2
FRI.	ISA. 8-10	2 TIM. 3-4	FRI.	PSA. 23-28	GAL. 3-6
SAT.	ISA. 11-13	TITUS 1-2	SAT.	PSA. 29-34	EPH. 1-4

TEN TIMES BETTER

WEEK 35 — TEN X BETTER

SUN.		PSALMS 58		SUN.	PSA. 91-92	REV. 1
MON.		PSALMS 59		MON.	PSA. 93-94	REV. 2
TUES.		PSALMS 60		TUES.	PSA. 95-96	REV. 3
WED.		PROVERBS 1		WED.	PSA. 97-98	REV. 4
THURS.		PROVERBS 2		THURS.	PSA. 99-100	REV. 5
FRI.		PROVERBS 3		FRI.	PSA. 101-102	REV. 6
SAT.		PROVERBS 4		SAT.	PSA. 103-104	REV. 7

SUN.	ISA. 14-16	TITUS 3 - PHM.		SUN.	PSA. 35-40	EPH. 5 - PHIL. 2
MON.	ISA. 15-17	HEB. 1-2		MON.	PSA. 41-46	PHIL. 3 - COL. 2
TUES.	ISA. 18-20	HEB. 3-4		TUES.	PSA. 47-52	COL. 3 - 1 THES. 2
WED.	ISA. 21-23	HEB. 5-6		WED.	PSA. 53-58	1 THES. 3 - 2 THES. 1
THURS.	ISA. 24-26	HEB. 7-8		THURS.	PSA. 59-64	2 THES. 2 - 1 TIM. 2
FRI.	ISA. 27-29	HEB. 9-10		FRI.	PSA. 65-70	1 TIM. 3-6
SAT.	ISA. 30-32	HEB. 11-12		SAT.	PSA. 71-76	2 TIM. 1-4

WEEK 36 — TEN X BETTER

SUN.	PROVERBS 5	PSA. 105-106	REV. 8
MON.	PROVERBS 6	PSA. 107-108	REV. 9
TUES.	PROVERBS 7	PSA. 109-110	REV. 10
WED.	PROVERBS 8	PSA. 111-112	REV. 11
THURS.	PROVERBS 9	PSA. 113-114	REV. 12
FRI.	PROVERBS 10	PSA. 115-116	REV. 13
SAT.	PROVERBS 11	PSA. 117-118	REV. 14

SUN.	ISA. 33-35	HEB. 13 – JAMES 1	PSA. 77-82
MON.	ISA. 36-38	JAMES 2-3	PSA. 83-88
TUES.	ISA. 39-41	JAMES 4-5	PSA. 89-94
WED.	ISA. 42-44	1 PET. 1-2	PSA. 95-100
THURS.	ISA. 45-47	1 PET. 3-4	PSA. 101-106
FRI.	ISA. 48-50	1 PET. 5 – 2 PET. 1	PSA. 107-112
SAT.	ISA. 51-53	2 PET. 2-3	PSA. 113-118

SUN.	TITUS – PHM.
MON.	HEB. 1-4
TUES.	HEB. 5-8
WED.	HEB. 9-12
THURS.	HEB. 13 – JAM. 3
FRI.	JAM. 4 – 1 PET. 2
SAT.	1 PET. 3 – 2 PET. 1

✗ WAYS TO BE A BETTER SERVANT

1. **SERVE WITH GLADNESS**
2. **SURRENDER**
3. **DIE TO SELF**
4. **SEE THE NEED**
5. **GIVE OF YOURSELF WHOLE HEARTEDLY**
6. **HONOR CHRIST**
7. **BUILD OTHERS**
8. **BE A BLESSING**
9. **RELINQUISH YOUR OPPORTUNITIES TO OTHERS**
10. **SERVE WITH CHARACTER**

-Dave Smith

> **THE BIBLE WILL KEEP YOU FROM SIN, OR SIN WILL KEEP YOU FROM THE BIBLE.**
>
> — D.L. MOODY

Nothing Is Impossible

EUGENE L. CLARK
EUGENE L. CLARK

Nothing is impossible when you put your trust in God;
Nothing is impossible when you're trusting in His Word.
Hearken to the voice of God to thee; "Is there anything too hard for Me?" Then put your trust in God alone and rest upon His Word; For ev-'ry-thing, O, ev-'ry-thing, yes ev-'ry-thing is possible with God.

NOTHING IS IMPOSSIBLE

Eugene L. Clark literally personified the title of his most famous song, "Nothing Is Impossible." Although his fingers once flew across the piano keyboard, he later became a victim of crippling arthritis and blindness. When it finally became impossible for Clark to continue playing the organ or piano, he requested that they bring to his bedside a dictating machine. With this marvelous electric invention and his most valuable possession, a keen mind, he continued to give to the world his beautiful musical offering. A note, a rest, a bar, and a dot at a time, the machine has recorded the product of his active mind—something that neither total blindness nor crippling arthritis could conquer. Hundreds of gospel songs and hymns, scores of choir arrangements, and three missionary cantatas have flowed through his dedicated heart and mind into the Christian world. His best-known song, "Nothing Is Impossible," was introduced in 1964. Clark was quick to credit his wife with a great deal of the success of his ministry. Her love, loyalty, and patience were invaluable assets to his work. The verse of Nothing Is Impossible reads:

> I read in the Bible the promise of God,
> That nothing for Him is too hard;
> Impossible things He has promised to do,
> If we faithfully trust in His Word.
>
> The word of the Lord is an anchor secure,
> When winds of uncertainty blow:
> Though man in his weakness may falter and fail,
> His Word will not fail us we know.
>
> All things are possible, this is His Word,
> Receive it 'tis written for you,
> Believe in His promises, God cannot fail,
> For what He has said He will do.

-MADE WHOLE OR MADE HOLY-

JOHN 6

John 6 perfectly describes our modern-day Christianity. At the beginning of the chapter, Jesus performs a miracle by feeding a crowd of thousands with just five loaves of bread and two fish. The people were so excited about the miracle that they spoke of forcing Jesus to rule as an earthly king. Jesus then departs to a mountain to avoid this and to be alone with God. The next day the crowd comes seeking after Jesus. When they find Him, they begin to question as to why He left them.

Wouldn't you think Jesus would be excited to see that many people seeking after Him? Wouldn't you think Jesus would be excited that people wanted to make Him a king over them? However, this was not the attitude of Christ. He immediately questions their motives and told them they only followed Him because they thought He could feed them. He tried to tell them that He is the bread of life, and they must believe on Him to obtain eternal life.

There have been so many times I've wondered how Jesus can perform such miracles for others, and yet so few people that stuck with Him through His death and after His resurrection. Why didn't they keep following Him? Jesus points it out in this chapter. They wanted to be made whole, but they don't want to be made holy. They wanted Him to be the Lord of the kingdom, but Jesus wanted to be the Lord of their heart. They wanted Jesus in their life so long as He met their temporary needs, but they didn't want Jesus in their heart to meet their eternal needs.

You want Jesus in your life because you think He is going to do for you. The second you realize that He wants your heart and you must believe in Him (not just what He can give you), then you will desert Him. You want Him to heal you and make you whole. But you don't want Him to make you holy. If you wanted to be holy, you would realize that trials in your life, give you an opportunity to be a better Christian. Suffering gives you the opportunity to walk closely with God.

If God took away your things, would you still serve Him? 1 Timothy 6:6, *"But godliness with contentment is great gain."* If you were like Joseph or Paul or Jeremiah at the bottom of the dungeon and all you had was God, would you be content and happy? If God never made you whole but wanted to make you holy, would you still love, follow, and seek Him? You don't become a better Christian by being blessed and made whole. You become a better Christian when God makes you holy.

-Brad Braudis

✗ POPULAR VERSES IN THE BIBLE

1) JOHN 3:16
For God so loved the world, that he gave his only begotten Son, that whosoever believeth in him should not perish, but have everlasting life.

2) MATTHEW 6:33
But seek ye first the kingdom of God, and his righteousness; and all these things shall be added unto you.

3) JEREMIAH 29:11
For I know the thoughts that I think toward you, saith the LORD, thoughts of peace, and not of evil, to give you an expected end.

4) ROMANS 8:28
And we know that all things work together for good to them that love God, to them who are the called according to his purpose.

5) ISAIAH 40:31
But they that wait upon the LORD shall renew their strength; they shall mount up with wings as eagles; they shall run, and not be weary; and they shall walk, and not faint.

6) 2 CORINTHIANS 5:17
Therefore if any man be in Christ, he is a new creature: old things are passed away; behold, all things are become new

7) MATTHEW 11:28
Come unto me, all ye that labour and are heavy laden, and I will give you rest.

8) MATTHEW 28:19
Go ye therefore, and teach all nations, baptizing them in the name of the Father, and of the Son, and of the Holy Ghost:

9) PHILIPIANS 4:13
I can do all things through Christ which strengtheneth me

10) PROVERBS 3:5
Trust in the Lord with all thine heart; and lean not unto thine own understanding.

WEEK 37 — TEN X BETTER

SUN.	PROVERBS 12	PSA. 119-120	REV. 15
MON.	PROVERBS 13	PSA. 121-122	REV. 16
TUES.	PROVERBS 14	PSA. 123-124	REV. 17
WED.	PROVERBS 15	PSA. 125-126	REV. 18
THURS.	PROVERBS 16	PSA. 127-128	REV. 19
FRI.	PROVERBS 17	PSA. 129-130	REV. 20
SAT.	PROVERBS 18	PSA. 131-32	REV. 21

SUN.	ISA. 54-56	PSA. 105-110	1 JHN. 1-2	2 PET. 2 - 1 JHN. 2
MON.	ISA. 57-59	PSA. 111-116	1 JHN. 3-4	1 JHN. 3 - 2 JHN.
TUES.	ISA. 60-62	PSA. 117-122	1 JHN. 5 - 2 JHN.	3 JHN. - REV. 2
WED.	ISA. 63-65	PSA. 123-128	3 JHN. - JUDE	REV. 3-6
THURS.	ISA. 66 - JER. 2	PSA. 129-134	REV. 1-2	REV. 7-10
FRI.	JER. 3-4	PSA. 135-140	REV. 3-4	REV. 11-14
SAT.	JER. 5-6	PSA. 141-146	REV. 5-6	REV. 15-18

WEEK 38 — TEN TIMES BETTER

SUN.	PROVERBS 19		SUN.	PSA. 133-134	REV. 22
MON.	PROVERBS 20		MON.	PSALMS 135-137	
TUES.	PROVERBS 21		TUES.	PSALMS 138-140	
WED.	PROVERBS 22		WED.	PSALMS 141-143	
THURS.	PROVERBS 23		THURS.	PSALMS 144-146	
FRI.	PROVERBS 24		FRI.	PSALMS 147-149	
SAT.	PROVERBS 25		SAT.	PSALMS 150 - PROVERBS 2	

SUN.	JER. 7-9	REV. 7-8	SUN.	PSA. 147 - PROV. 2	REV. 19-22
MON.	JER. 10-12	REV. 9-10	MON.	PROV. 3-8	MATT. 1-4
TUES.	JER. 13-15	REV. 11-12	TUES.	PROV. 9-14	MATT. 5-8
WED.	JER. 16-18	REV. 13-14	WED.	PROV. 15-20	MATT. 9-12
THURS.	JER. 19-21	REV. 15-16	THURS.	PROV. 21-26	MATT. 13-16
FRI.	JER. 22-24	REV. 17-18	FRI.	PROV. 27 - ECC. 1	MATT. 17-20
SAT.	JER. 25-27	REV. 19-20	SAT.	ECC. 2-7	MATT. 21-24

WEEK

SUN.	PROVERBS 3-5
MON.	PROVERBS 6-8
TUES.	PROVERBS 9-11
WED.	PROVERBS 12-14
THURS.	PROVERBS 15-17
FRI.	PROVERBS 18-20
SAT.	PROVERBS 21-23

SUN.	PROVERBS 26
MON.	PROVERBS 27
TUES.	PROVERBS 28
WED.	PROVERBS 29
THURS.	PROVERBS 30
FRI.	PROVERBS 31
SAT.	PSALMS 61

TEN x BETTER — 39

TEN TIMES BETTER

SUN.	ECC. 8 - SONG. 1	MATT. 25-28
MON.	SONG. 2-7	MARK 1-4
TUES.	SONG. 8 - ISA. 5	MARK 5-8
WED.	ISA. 6-11	MARK 9-12
THURS.	ISA. 12-17	MARK 13-16
FRI.	ISA. 18-23	LUKE 1-4
SAT.	ISA. 24-29	LUKE 5-8

SUN.	JER. 28-30	REV. 21-22
MON.	JER. 31-33	MATT. 1-2
TUES.	JER. 34-36	MATT. 3-4
WED.	JER. 37-39	MATT. 5-6
THURS.	JER. 40-42	MATT. 7-8
FRI.	JER. 43-45	MATT. 9-10
SAT.	JER. 46-48	MATT. 11-12

TEN X BETTER

TEN TIMES BETTER — 40

WEEK

SUN.	PSALMS 62
MON.	PSALMS 63
TUES.	PSALMS 64
WED.	PSALMS 65
THURS.	PSALMS 66
FRI.	PSALMS 67
SAT.	PSALMS 68

SUN.	PROVERBS 24-26
MON.	PROVERBS 27-29
TUES.	PROVERBS 30 - ECC. 1
WED.	ECCLESIASTES 2-4
THURS.	ECCLESIASTES 5-7
FRI.	ECCLESIASTES 8-10
SAT.	ECCLESIASTES 11-12; ISAIAH 1

SUN.	JER. 49-51
MON.	JER. 52 - LAM. 2
TUES.	LAM. 3-5
WED.	EZEK. 1-3
THURS.	EZEK. 4-6
FRI.	EZEK. 7-9
SAT.	EZEK. 10-12

SUN.	ISA. 30-35
MON.	ISA. 36-41
TUES.	ISA. 42-47
WED.	ISA. 48-53
THURS.	ISA. 54-59
FRI.	ISA. 60-65
SAT.	ISA. 66 - JER. 5

SUN.	MATT. 13-14
MON.	MATT. 15-16
TUES.	MATT. 17-18
WED.	MATT. 19-20
THURS.	MATT. 21-22
FRI.	MATT. 23-24
SAT.	MATT. 25-26

SUN.	JOHN 13-16
MON.	JOHN 17-20
TUES.	JOHN 21 - ACTS 3
WED.	ACTS 4-7
THURS.	ACTS 8-11
FRI.	ACTS 12-15
SAT.	ACTS 16-19

X WAYS TO BE A BETTER TEAMMATE

1. HAVE A GOOD ATTITUDE
2. BE COACHABLE
3. BE AN ENCOURAGER
4. GIVE IT YOUR ALL IN PRACTICE
5. HAVE GOOD BODY LANGUAGE
6. HAVE PASSION
7. PERSERVERE
8. BE DISCIPLINED
9. WORK HARD
10. TRUST

-Rich Carr

> **"I'D RATHER DIE IN THE WILL OF GOD, THAN TO LIVE OUTSIDE OF IT.**

JACK HYLES

-WHAT IS THE WILL OF GOD-

1 JOHN 2:15-17

One of the most confusing subjects for many young people, is the will of God. It's confusing enough, then you hear so many versions of what it is. People will talk of God speaking to their heart as if He was really speaking. They will talk about the Lord leading them. Some will shout that they have received a word from the Lord. My hope is to make it simple for anyone reading today.

Eph 5:17 ,"*Wherefore be ye not unwise, but understanding what the will of the Lord is.*"

THE WILL OF GOD IS THE WORD OF GOD. (Matt. 4:4; Heb. 5:13; 2 Tim. 3:16)
Anything the Bible commands you to do is the will of God. Anything the Bible forbids you to do is the will of God. Where the Bible does not clearly and definitively address something, it gives you principles that can help guide your decisions and make wise choices. Obedience to the Word of God is essential to living in the will of God.

THE WILL OF GOD IS GROWING IN GOD. (Luke 3:6-9)
Is there something that would hinder your growth spiritually? Is there something that would keep you from getting closer to God in your walk with Him? Many people have asked if they should take a certain job. My question, "Does it keep you from church services?" If so, it goes against the clear will of God (Hebrews 10:25). Should I move to this area where there is a good job? Is there a good, Bible-preaching church there? If not, then it would severely hinder your Christian growth.

THE WILL OF GOD IS DETERMINED BY YOUR POTENTIAL. (Luke 3:8-9)
The servant wanted to work with the tree because he believed it had potential. Every believer has been given a certain amount of potential as in the parable of the talents (Matthew 25:15-30). You may ask, "How do I know my potential?" You Look at your abilities – Matthew 25:15 ...to every man according to his several ability....

YOU INCREASE YOUR POTENTIAL TO DO MORE FOR GOD BY INCREASING YOUR ABILITIES. (Matthew 25:21)
Often, we don't know our potential, but we do know our abilities. What can you do right now? Could you sing in the choir? Do you have the time to go soulwinning? You can't talk, but can you go as a silent partner? You may not be able to captain the bus route, but can you help pass out candy? Do what you can so you can do more. (Philippians 4:13)

-Brad Braudis

X THINGS TEENS SHOULD SAY

1. HELLO.
2. THANK YOU.
3. PLEASE.
4. HERE, TAKE MY SEAT.
5. MY PLEASURE.
6. LET ME HELP YOU WITH THAT.
7. MY NAME IS [NAME].
8. HAVE A GREAT DAY!
9. I LOVE YOU.
10. I'M SORRY.

-William Davis

Set My Soul Afire

GENE BARTLETT

1. Set my soul a-fire, Lord, for Thy Ho-ly Word, Burn it deep with-in me,
2. Set my soul a-fire, Lord, for the lost in sin, Give to me a pas-sion
3. Set my soul a-fire, Lord, in my dai-ly life, Far too long I've wandered

let Your voice be heard; Mil-lions grope in dark-ness in this day and hour,
as I seek to win; Help me not to fal-ter, nev-er let me fail,
in this day of strife; Noth-ing else will mat-ter but to live for Thee,

I will be Your wit-ness, fill me with Thy pow'r.
Fill me with Thy Spir-it, let Thy will pre-vail. Set my soul a-fire, Lord, set my
I will be Your wit-ness as You live in me.

soul a-fire, Make my life a wit-ness of Thy sav-ing pow'r. Mil-lions grope in

dark-ness, wait-ing for Thy Word, Set my soul a-fire Lord, Set my soul a-fire.

SET MY SOUL AFIRE

Gene Bartlett Jr. wrote "Set My Soul Afire," as a prayer to God that he would keep his heart from becoming complacent. In Leviticus 6:9, 11-12, the Lord tells Moses to instruct Aaron and his sons to keep the fire of the alter burning all day and night. He places emphasis on the importance of not letting the fire go out. Undoubtedly it was hard to accomplish this task, as the land in that day was not known for its lush forests and firewood. The priests in that day had to have the alter on their minds and make it a constant effort to keep it burning. Just as God commanded Aaron and his sons to keep the alter burning, He wants us to keep our soul afire for Him.

Often the "fire" or zeal for God in our lives can be hidden or diminished by hardships and sometimes even sin in our life. To keep from growing complacent we must set a prayer at the forefront of our heart that requests for the Holy Spirit's power to fall upon us and kindle a fire in our soul that won't easily be put out. Our prayer should be that God make us a light in a darkened world. We have the opportunity and ability to make a difference in this world if we just let our fire for Jesus be shown. "Millions grope in darkness, waiting for Thy Word, Set my soul afire Lord, Set my soul afire!"

WEEK 41

TEN

SUN.	PSALMS 69	SUN.	EZEK. 13-15	MATT. 27-28
MON.	PSALMS 70	MON.	EZEK. 16-18	MARK 1-2
TUES.	PSALMS 71	TUES.	EZEK. 19-21	MARK 3-4
WED.	PSALMS 72	WED.	EZEK. 22-24	MARK 5-6
THURS.	PSALMS 73	THURS.	EZEK. 25-27	MARK 7-8
FRI.	PSALMS 74	FRI.	EZEK. 28-30	MARK 9-10
SAT.	PSALMS 75	SAT.	EZEK. 31-33	MARK 11-12

BETTER

SUN.	ISAIAH 2-4	SUN.	JER. 6-11	ACTS 20-23
MON.	ISAIAH 5-7	MON.	JER. 12-17	ACTS 24-27
TUES.	ISAIAH 8-10	TUES.	JER. 18-23	ACTS 28 - ROM. 3
WED.	ISAIAH 11-13	WED.	JER. 24-29	ROM. 4-7
THURS.	ISAIAH 14-16	THURS.	JER. 30-35	ROM. 8-11
FRI.	ISAIAH 17-19	FRI.	JER. 36-41	ROM. 12-15
SAT.	ISAIAH 20-22	SAT.	JER. 42-47	ROM. 16 - 1 COR. 3

TEN TIMES BETTER

WEEK 42

TEN X BETTER

SUN.	PSALMS 76	SUN.	ISAIAH 23-25
MON.	PSALMS 77	MON.	ISAIAH 26-28
TUES.	PSALMS 78	TUES.	ISAIAH 29-31
WED.	PSALMS 79	WED.	ISAIAH 32-34
THURS.	PSALMS 80	THURS.	ISAIAH 35-37
FRI.	PSALMS 81	FRI.	ISAIAH 38-40
SAT.	PSALMS 82	SAT.	ISAIAH 41-43

SUN.	EZEK. 34-36	MARK 13-14	
MON.	EZEK. 37-39	MARK 15-16	
TUES.	EZEK. 40-42	LUKE 1-2	
WED.	EZEK. 43-45	LUKE 3-4	
THURS.	EZEK. 46-48	LUKE 5-6	
FRI.	DAN. 1-3	LUKE 7-8	
SAT.	DAN. 4-6	LUKE 9-10	

SUN.	JER. 48 - LAM 1	1 COR. 4-7
MON.	LAM. 2 - EZEK. 2	1 COR. 8-11
TUES.	EZEK. 3-8	1 COR. 12-15
WED.	EZEK. 9-14	1 COR. 16 - 2 COR. 3
THURS.	EZEK. 15-20	2 COR. 4-7
FRI.	EZEK. 21-26	2 COR. 8-11
SAT.	EZEK. 27-32	2 COR. 12 - GAL. 2

WEEK 43 — TEN X BETTER

Week

SUN.	PSALMS 83	SUN.	ISAIAH 44-46
MON.	PSALMS 84	MON.	ISAIAH 47-49
TUES.	PSALMS 85	TUES.	ISAIAH 50-52
WED.	PSALMS 86	WED.	ISAIAH 53-55
THURS.	PSALMS 87	THURS.	ISAIAH 56-58
FRI.	PSALMS 88	FRI.	ISAIAH 59-61
SAT.	PSALMS 89	SAT.	ISAIAH 62-64

Ten X Better

SUN.	DAN. 7-9	LUKE 11-12	EZEK. 33-38	GAL. 3-6
MON.	DAN. 10-12	LUKE 13-14	EZEK. 39-44	EPH. 1-4
TUES.	HOS. 1-3	LUKE 15-16	EZEK. 45 - DAN. 2	EPH. 5 - PHIL. 2
WED.	HOS. 4-6	LUKE 17-18	DAN. 3-8	PHIL. 3 - COL. 2
THURS.	HOS. 7-9	LUKE 19-20	DAN. 9 - HOS. 2	COL. 3 - 1 THES. 2
FRI.	HOS. 10-12	LUKE 21-22	HOS. 3-8	1 THES. 3 - 2 THES. 1
SAT.	HOS. 13 - JOEL 1	LUKE 23-24	HOS. 9-14	2 THES. 2 - 1 TIM. 2

WEEK 44 — TEN X BETTER

Day	TEN		BETTER	
SUN.	PSALMS 90	JOEL 2 - AMOS 1	ISAIAH 65 - JEREMIAH 1	JOEL - AMOS 3
MON.	PSALMS 91	AMOS 2-4	JEREMIAH 2-4	AMOS 4-9
TUES.	PSALMS 92	AMOS 5-7	JEREMIAH 5-7	OBD. - MIC. 1
WED.	PSALMS 93	AMOS 8 - OBD.	JEREMIAH 8-10	MIC. 2-7
THURS.	PSALMS 94	JON. 1-3	JEREMIAH 11-13	NAH. - HAB.
FRI.	PSALMS 95	JON. 4 - MIC. 2	JEREMIAH 14-16	ZEPH. 1 - ZECH. 1
SAT.	PSALMS 96	MIC. 3-5	JEREMIAH 17-19	ZECH. 2-7

Day	TEN (John)	BETTER
SUN.	JOHN 1-2	1 TIM. 3-6
MON.	JOHN 3-4	2 TIM. 1-4
TUES.	JOHN 5-6	TITUS - PHM.
WED.	JOHN 7-8	HEB. 1-4
THURS.	JOHN 9-10	HEB. 5-8
FRI.	JOHN 11-12	HEB. 9-12
SAT.	JOHN 13-14	HEB. 13 - JAS. 3

TEN TIMES BETTER

✘ WAYS TO BE A BETTER CHOIR MEMBER

1. **SING FOR GOD NOT YOURSELF**
2. **UNDERSTAND EVERY VOICE IS IMPORTANT**
3. **WORK TOGETHER WITH OTHER SINGERS**
4. **FAITHFULLY ATTEND CHOIR PRACTICE**
5. **LISTEN TO GOOD CHOIR ARRANGEMENTS**
6. **LEARN YOUR PART QUICKLY**
7. **SING WITH CONFIDENCE, HELPING OTHERS**
8. **WATCH THE DIRECTOR**
9. **KEEP GOOD FACIAL EXPRESSIONS**
10. **LOOK UP AND SING OUT**

-Troy Young

> "THE LORD GETS HIS BEST SOLDIERS FROM THE HIGHLAND OF AFFLICTION.

— CHARLES SPURGEON

Stand Up, Stand Up for Jesus

1. Stand up, stand up for Jesus, ye soldiers of the cross;
lift high His royal banner, it must not suffer loss.
From victory unto victory, His army shall he lead,
till every foe is vanquished, and Christ is Lord indeed.

2. Stand up, stand up for Jesus, the trumpet call obey;
forth to the mighty conflict, in this His glorious day.
Ye who are brave now serve Him against unnumbered foes;
let courage rise with danger, and strength to strength oppose.

3. Stand up, stand up for Jesus, stand in His strength alone;
the arm of flesh will fail you, ye dare not trust your own.
Put on the gospel armor, each piece put on with prayer;
where duty calls or danger, be never wanting there.

4. Stand up, stand up for Jesus, the strife will not be long;
this day the noise of battle, the next the victor's song.
To those who vanquish evil a crown of life shall be;
they with the King of Glory shall reign eternally.

STAND UP, STAND UP FOR JESUS

"Stand Up, Stand Up for Jesus" is an American Christian hymn. It was written by George Duffield, Jr. in 1858 and is based on the dying words of Dudley Atkins Tyng. In 1858, minister George Duffield, Jr. was an associate of Dudley Atkins Tyng, who had recently been removed from his local church community for speaking against slavery. Duffield assisted Tyng in supporting a revival of evangelicalism in Pennsylvania.

In March 1858, Tyng gave a sermon at a YMCA meeting of over 5,000 men on Exodus 10:11, "Go now ye that are men, and serve the Lord", converting over 1,000 men listening in the crowd. The following month, Tyng was maimed in a farming accident. Before he died a few days after the accident he told his father "Tell my brethren of the ministry, wherever you meet them, to stand up for Jesus." Duffield then wrote the hymn based on those words, and also incorporated the phrase "Ye that are men now serve Him" from Tyng's memorable sermon the month before he died. At a memorial service for Tyng, Duffield gave a sermon based on Ephesians 6:14, "Stand therefore, having your loins girt about with truth, and having on the breastplate of righteousness;", and ended it by reciting the new hymn he had written as a tribute. The hymn was first brought into public knowledge through leaflets printed by the superintendent of the local Christian school containing the words of the hymn. One of these leaflets ended up being published in a Baptist newspaper, and "Stand Up, Stand Up for Jesus," was published in *The Church Psalmist* in 1859. After first publication, the hymn was popular and was sung by both the Union and Confederate soldiers in the American Civil War. The hymn also became popular among British revivalists, and within public schools in England.

-FINISHING WELL-

2 TIMOTHY 4:7

In II Timothy 4:7 Paul, the veteran preacher of the gospel, is now at his place of his "departure" from this life and he writes to younger Timothy to encourage him and challenge him in the work of the ministry. Among other things of his challenge he tells Timothy three things that kept him on track to finish well his race of life. Let's look at what these three things were.

1. HE FOUGHT A GOOD FIGHT

Paul means that his work was not an easy task. He had opposition. He had to Fight to get it done! (II Timothy 2:3)(II Corinthians 4:8-10) Paul's mission in life was not an easy task and neither will ours be. He fought the feelings of his flesh, the temptations of the world and the attacks of the devil.

2. HE FINISHED THE COURSE

As I understand the word "course" I take it to mean that each part of the Race (his life) was a course. As he completed each step or course that allowed him yet another step or course to complete. Times of imprisonment were a course. Times of delay were a course. Times of working to make tents were a course. Each of his courses in life made up his race and as he completed his courses he completed his race in the will of God. I say to you today, finish the current course of your life, finish the work you have to do today.

3. HE KEPT THE FAITH

Paul's faith was tested on every hand. There were times that he wanted to replace his faith with a fear. However, Paul determined to maintain his faith in God. (James 1:2-4) Sometimes we are challenged in the decisions of faith. Decisions made in Faith are always challenged in times of doubt! Whatever we initiate in faith we should never recapitulate in doubt. The desires of our faith are challenged by our weaknesses and weariness. Paul stayed on track and he pressed toward the "Mark." The directions of our faith are challenged by surprises and confusions of life and faith.

I have been a pastor for 32 years. I grew up in a preachers home. I have seen the Lord do some mighty wonderful things. And yet, they have not been easy to accomplish. My life could be summed up like:

A FIGHT – many oppositions to right
FINISH EACH COURSE – step by step.
KEEP FAITH – Never giving in to Fears – staying strong in the promises of God!

I say to you today, **FIGHT, FINISH AND KEEP THE FAITH!**

-Pastor Jeff Fugate

✘ THINGS JESUS PRAYED FOR

1. **MATTHEW 6-10** - *For God's Will*
2. **JOHN 17:3** - *For us to know God*
3. **JOHN 17:17-19** - *For us to be sanctified*
4. **JOHN 17:23** - *The Lost to be Saved*
5. **JOHN 12:28** - *The Father to be Glorified*
6. **MATTHEW 6:11** - *Daily Provisions*
7. **LUKE 23:34** - *Forgivenss*
8. **LUKE 22:42** - *Yielding Life to God*
9. **JOHN 17:15** - *For Leaders*
10. **JOHN 17:9-11, 20** - *For His Friends*

WEEK 45 — TEN X BETTER

SUN.		PSALMS 97
MON.		PSALMS 98
TUES.		PSALMS 99
WED.		PSALMS 100
THURS.		PSALMS 101
FRI.		PSALMS 102
SAT.		PSALMS 103

SUN.		JEREMIAH 20-22
MON.		JEREMIAH 23-25
TUES.		JEREMIAH 26-28
WED.		JEREMIAH 29-31
THURS.		JEREMIAH 32-34
FRI.		JEREMIAH 35-37
SAT.		JEREMIAH 38-40

TEN

SUN.	MIC. 6 - NAH. 1	JOHN 15-16
MON.	NAH. 2 - HAB. 1	JOHN 17-18
TUES.	HAB. 2 - ZEPH. 1	JOHN 19-20
WED.	ZEPH. 2 - HAG. 1	JOHN 21 - ACTS 1
THURS.	HAG. 2 - ZECH. 2	ACTS 2-3
FRI.	ZECH. 3-5	ACTS 4-5
SAT.	ZECH. 6-8	ACTS 6-7

BETTER

SUN.	ZECH. 8-13	JAS. 4 - 1 PET. 2
MON.	ZECH. 14 - MAL. 4	1 PET. 3 - 2 PET. 1
TUES.	PSA. 1-6	2 PET. 2 - 1 JHN. 2
WED.	PSA. 7-12	1 JHN. 3 - 2 JHN.
THURS.	PSA. 13-18	3 JHN. - REV. 2
FRI.	PSA. 19-24	REV. 3-6
SAT.	PSA. 25-30	REV. 7-10

WEEK 46 — TEN TIMES BETTER

SUN.		JEREMIAH 41-43
MON.		JEREMIAH 44-46
TUES.		JEREMIAH 47-49
WED.		JEREMIAH 50-52
THURS.		LAMENTATIONS 1-3
FRI.		LAMENTATIONS 4 - EZEKIEL 1
SAT.		EZEKIEL 2-4

SUN.	PSA. 31-36	REV. 11-14
MON.	PSA. 37-41	REV. 15-18
TUES.	PSA. 42-47	REV. 19-22
WED.	PSA. 48-53	MATT. 1-4
THURS.	PSA. 54-59	MATT. 5-8
FRI.	PSA. 60-65	MATT. 9-12
SAT.	PSA. 66-71	MATT. 13-16

SUN.		PSALMS 104
MON.		PSALMS 105
TUES.		PSALMS 106
WED.		PSALMS 107
THURS.		PSALMS 108
FRI.		PSALMS 109
SAT.		PSALMS 110

SUN.	ZECH. 9-11	ACTS 8-9
MON.	ZECH. 12-14	ACTS 10-11
TUES.	MAL. 1-3	ACTS 12-13
WED.	MAL. 4; GEN. 1-2	ACTS 14-15
THURS.	GEN. 3-5	ACTS 16-17
FRI.	GEN. 6-8	ACTS 18-19
SAT.	GEN. 9-11	ACTS 20-21

WEEK 47 — TEN X BETTER

	TEN			BETTER	
SUN.	GEN. 12-14	PSALMS 111	ACTS 22-23	SUN.	EZEKIEL 5-7	PSA. 72-77	MATT. 17-20
MON.	GEN. 15-17	PSALMS 112	ACTS 24-25	MON.	EZEKIEL 8-10	PSA. 78-83	MATT. 21-24
TUES.	GEN. 18-20	PSALMS 113	ACTS 26-27	TUES.	EZEKIEL 11-13	PSA. 84-89	MATT. 25-28
WED.	GEN. 21-23	PSALMS 114	ACTS 28 - ROM. 1	WED.	EZEKIEL 14-16	PSA. 90-95	MARK 1-4
THURS.	GEN. 24-26	PSALMS 115	ROM. 2-3	THURS.	EZEKIEL 17-19	PSA. 96-102	MARK 5-8
FRI.	GEN. 27-29	PSALMS 116	ROM. 4-5	FRI.	EZEKIEL 20-22	PSA. 103-108	MARK 9-12
SAT.	GEN. 30-32	PSALMS 117	ROM. 6-7	SAT.	EZEKIEL 23-25	PSA. 109-114	MARK 13-16

TEN TIMES BETTER

TEN × BETTER

WEEK 48

SUN.	PSALMS 118		SUN.	PSA. 115-120		LUKE 1-4
MON.	PSALMS 119		MON.	PSA. 121-126	EZEKIEL 26-28	LUKE 5-8
TUES.	PSALMS 120		TUES.	PSA. 127-132	EZEKIEL 29-31	LUKE 9-12
WED.	PSALMS 121		WED.	PSA. 133-138	EZEKIEL 32-34	LUKE 13-16
THURS.	PSALMS 122		THURS.	PSA. 139-144	EZEKIEL 35-37	JOHN 1-4
FRI.	PSALMS 123		FRI.	PSA. 145-150	EZEKIEL 38-40	JOHN 5-8
SAT.	PSALMS 124		SAT.	PROV. 1-6	EZEKIEL 41-43	JOHN 9-12
					EZEKIEL 44-46	

SUN.	GEN. 33-35	ROM. 8-10	
MON.	GEN. 36-38	ROM. 11-13	
TUES.	GEN. 39-41	ROM. 14-16	
WED.	GEN. 42-44	ACTS 1-2	
THURS.	GEN. 45-47	ACTS 3-4	
FRI.	GEN. 48-50	ACTS 5-6	
SAT.	1 SAM. 1-3	ACTS 7-8	

✘ WAYS TO BE A BETTER SINGER

1. CONTEMPLATE THE PURPOSE OF THE SONG
2. CONCENTRATE ON THE MESSAGE
3. PRACTICE MORE THAN NECESSARY
4. SING FROM YOUR DIAPHRAGM
5. WORK ON YOUR BREATHING
6. EXCERCISE YOUR DIAPHRAGM
7. HUM THE SONG TO LOOSEN YOUR VOICE
8. BE AROUND EXPERIENCED SINGERS
9. DON'T LISTEN TO CONTEMPORARY STYLES
10. PRAY AND DEPEND ON GOD

-Joel Fugate

> "I HAVE HAD MORE TROUBLE WITH MYSELF THAN WITH ANY OTHER MAN I HAVE EVER MET."
>
> — D.L. MOODY

-THERE IS NO FUN IN THE FAR COUNTRY-

LUKE 15:11-24

This parable is a story of two brothers. Both were in the same home, had the same training and the same opportunities. Both were heirs to a substantial inheritance. One was appreciative for his wonderful opportunity. The other was not. The younger wanted his inheritance NOW. He was tired of the work, the responsibility, the chores and having his parents tell him what to do. He decided to take his portion of the inheritance now and live to enjoy his life. With all of the money he received from his parents, he did not have to work; he had time for fun and relaxation. As we know, he "wasted his substance with riotous living." (Luke 15:13). He chose to "enjoy the pleasures of sin" (Hebrews 11:25) in that riotous life style that undoubtedly included alcohol, any other drugs available at the time, wicked "friends" and immorality.

However, he soon learned that those pleasures only lasted "for a season." (Hebrews 11:25). When his money was gone, so were all of the pleasures. Now he was miserable – and learning that "there is no fun in the far country." He came home, asked his father for mercy, and was received.

However, even though he was received by his father, given his needs and the opportunity to work on the farm again – he had still lost his inheritance! Sin always costs.

On the other hand, the elder son had stayed faithful, worked hard, been obedient and a good son.

There is no fun in the far country. Do not waste your inheritance.

-Jim Jorgensen

X THINGS TEENS NEED TO KNOW

1. HOW TO WASH THEIR CLOTHES
2. HOW TO COOK A MEAL
3. HOW TO EARN THEIR OWN MONEY
4. HOW TO LOVE THEIR PARENTS
5. HOW TO REMAIN PURE
6. HOW TO PUT OTHERS FIRST
7. HOW TO MIND THEIR MANNERS
8. HOW TO ASK FOR HELP WHEN THEY REALLY NEED IT
9. HOW TO SEE THE WORLD IN PERSPECTIVE
10. HOW TO BE WISE

-William Davis

Take My Life and Let It Be

Frances R. Havergal
H.A. Cesar Malan

1. Take my life and let it be Consecrated, Lord, to Thee; Take my moments and my days, Let them flow in ceaseless praise, Let them flow in ceaseless praise.

2. Take my hands and let them move At the impulse of Thy love; Take my feet and let them be Swift and beautiful for Thee, Swift and beautiful for Thee.

3. Take my voice and let me sing Always, only, for my King; Take my lips and let them be Filled with messages from Thee, Filled with messages from Thee.

4. Take my silver and my gold Not a mite would I withhold; Take my intellect and use Ev'ry pow'r as Thou shalt choose, Ev'ry pow'r as Thou shalt choose.

5. Take my will and make it Thine It shall be no longer mine; Take my heart it is Thine own, It shall be Thy royal throne, It shall be Thy royal throne.

6. Take my love; my Lord, I pour At Thy feet its treasure store; Take myself and I will be Ever, only, all for Thee, Ever, only, all for Thee.

TAKE MY LIFE AND LET IT BE

Frances Ridely Havergal (1836-1879) has provided us with one of the classic hymns of Christian commitment. Known as the "consecration poet," Havergal attempted to live a life fully consecrated to Christ and to those she saw in any physical or spiritual need. Havergal's spirituality began early in her life, memorizing passages in the Bible at age 4 and writing songs by age seven.

Frances went to a house full of prisoners for a period of five days when she was older in age. She tells how she prayed that by the time she left the house, the Lord would give her strength to see all the prisoners saved. After only a couple of days, every prisoner along with the hosts of the house, received salvation. As she lay in bed awake late one night after thinking about how God gave her the power to witness, she wrote down the words, "Ever, Only, All for Thee."

"Take my life and let it be," was Frances Havergal's constant prayer of self consecration to Christ. She wanted to be fully used of God to lead the lost to salvation. She said that she would give all she had, even silver and gold, to reach others for Christ.

WEEK 49 — TEN X BETTER

SUN.	PSALMS 125		SUN.	EZEKIEL 47-48 ; DANIEL 1
MON.	PSALMS 126		MON.	DANIEL 2-4
TUES.	PSALMS 127		TUES.	DANIEL 5-7
WED.	PSALMS 128		WED.	DANIEL 8-10
THURS.	PSALMS 129		THURS.	DANIEL 11-12 ; HOSEA 1
FRI.	PSALMS 130		FRI.	HOSEA 2-4
SAT.	PSALMS 131		SAT.	HOSEA 5-7

SUN.	1 SAM. 4-6	ACTS 9-10	SUN.	PROV. 7-12	JOHN 13-16
MON.	1 SAM. 7-9	ACTS 11-12	MON.	PROV. 13-18	JOHN 17-20
TUES.	1 SAM. 10-12	ACTS 13-14	TUES.	PROV. 19-24	JOHN 21 - ACTS 3
WED.	1 SAM. 13-15	ACTS 15-16	WED.	PROV. 25-30	ACTS 4-7
THURS.	1 SAM. 16-18	ACTS 17-18	THURS.	PROV. 31 - ECC. 5	ACTS 8-11
FRI.	1 SAM. 19-21	ACTS 19-20	FRI.	ECC. 6-11	ACTS 12-15
SAT.	1 SAM. 22-24	ACTS 21-22	SAT.	ECC 12 ; ISA. 1-5	ACTS 16-19

WEEK

SUN.		HOSEA 8-10
MON.		HOSEA 11-13
TUES.		HOSEA 14 ; JOEL 1-2
WED.		JOEL 3 ; AMOS 1-2
THURS.		AMOS 3-5
FRI.		AMOS 6-8
SAT.		AMOS 9 - JONAH 1

SUN.		PSALMS 132
MON.		PSALMS 133
TUES.		PSALMS 134
WED.		PSALMS 135
THURS.		PSALMS 136
FRI.		PSALMS 137
SAT.		PSALMS 138

TEN X BETTER — 50 (TEN TIMES BETTER)

SUN.	ISA. 6-11	ACTS 20-23
MON.	ISA. 12-17	ACTS 24-27
TUES.	ISA. 18-23	ACTS 28 - ROM. 3
WED.	ISA. 24-29	ROM. 4-7
THURS.	ISA. 30-35	ROM. 8-11
FRI.	ISA. 36-41	ROM. 12-15
SAT.	ISA. 42-47	ROM. 16 - 1 COR. 3

SUN.	1 SAM. 24-26	ACTS 23-24
MON.	1 SAM. 27-29	ACTS 25-26
TUES.	1 SAM. 30-31 ; PROV. 1	ACTS 27-28
WED.	PROV. 2-4	ROM. 1-2
THURS.	PROV. 5-7	ROM. 3-4
FRI.	PROV. 8-10	ROM. 5-6
SAT.	PROV. 11-13	ROM. 7-8

WEEK 51 — TEN X BETTER

SUN.	PSALMS 139	PROV. 14-16	ROM. 9-10
MON.	PSALMS 140	PROV. 17-19	ROM. 11-12
TUES.	PSALMS 141	PROV. 20-22	ROM. 13-14
WED.	PSALMS 142	PROV. 23-25	ROM. 15-16
THURS.	PSALMS 143	PROV. 26-28	GAL. 1-2
FRI.	PSALMS 144	PROV. 29-31	GAL. 3-4
SAT.	PSALMS 145	ECC. 1-3	GAL. 5-6

SUN.	JONAH 2-4	ISA. 48-53	1 COR. 4-7
MON.	MICAH 1-3	ISA. 54-59	1 COR. 8-11
TUES.	MICAH 4-6	ISA. 60-65	1 COR. 16 - 2 COR. 3
WED.	MICAH 7 - NAHUM 2	ISA. 66 - JER. 1-5	2 COR. 4-7
THURS.	NAHUM 3 - HABAKKUK 2	JER. 6-11	2 COR. 8-11
FRI.	HABAKKUK 3 - ZEPHANIAH 2	JER. 12-17	2 COR. 12 - GAL. 2
SAT.	ZEPHANIAH 3 - HAGGAI 2	JER. 18-23	GAL. 3-6

TEN TIMES BETTER — WEEK 52

	Column A	Column B
SUN.	PSALMS 146	ZECHARIAH 1-3
MON.	PSALMS 147	ZECHARIAH 4-6
TUES.	PSALMS 148	ZECHARIAH 7-9
WED.	PSALMS 149	ZECHARIAH 10-12
THURS.	PSALMS 150	ZECHARIAH 13 - MALACHI 1
FRI.	PROVERBS 31	MALACHI 2-4
SAT.	ECCLESIASTES 12	TITUS 1-3

	Column A	Column B	Column C	Column D
SUN.	ECC. 4-6	EPH. 1-2	JER. 24-29	EPH. 1-4
MON.	ECC. 7-9	EPH. 3-4	JER. 30-35	EPH. 5 - PHIL.
TUES.	ECC. 10-12	EPH. 5-6	JER. 36-41	COL. 1-4
WED.	DAN. 1-3	PHIL. 1-2	JER. 42-47	1 TIM. 1-4
THURS.	DAN. 4-6	PHIL. 3-4	JER. 48 - LAM. 1	1 TIM. 5 - 2 TIM. 2
FRI.	DAN. 7-9	COL. 1-2	LAM. 2-5 ; JOEL 1-2	2 TIM. 3-4 ; JAS. 1-2
SAT.	DAN. 10-12	COL. 3-4	JOEL 3 ; OBD. - JON.	JAS. 3-5 ; JUDE

Victory in Jesus

E. M. BARTLETT   E. M. BARTLETT

O vic-to-ry in Je-sus, My Sav-ior, for-ev-er, He sought me and bought me With His re-deem-ing blood; He loved me ere I knew Him And all my love is due Him, He plunged me to vic-to-ry, Be-neath the cleans-ing flood.

VICTORY IN JESUS

Eugene Bartlett was born on Christmas Eve 1885 in Waynesville, Missouri. He gave his life to Christ early in life. He demonstrated a strong voice and a love for music in his childhood. After attending school in Tennessee and Missouri, Bartlett took to the road, teaching Singing Schools and writing songs. His words and tunes ("Everybody will be happy over there" and "Just a little while") were popular in the Singing Conventions of the early 1900s.

Bartlett was also a successful businessman. He established his career working for the Central Music Company, in Arkansas, which published shaped-note songbooks. Bartlett would later establish the Hartford Music Institute, which trained hundreds of teachers and musicians each year. One day in 1926 a penniless young man showed up at the Hartford Music Institute, and finding Bartlett in his office, said, "Mr. Bartlett, I hear that you'll teach a fella how to sing and how to write music. I've come to learn and I understand I don't have to have any money." Bartlett asked the young man if he had money for room and board. He didn't. "Well, in that case," said Bartlett, "you better go over to my house and board." The young man, Albert E. Brumley, later became the dean of southern gospel publishing and the author of "I'll Fly Away."

E. M. Bartlett suffered a stroke in 1939, that left him partially paralyzed. He was to live only two more years after the incident. During his illness he devoted his time to studying the Bible and counting his blessings. The last of his eight hundred hymns and songs was the most difficult to write due to his impaired condition. It came painfully, phrase by phrase and note by note. It was the culmination of his like's work – *"Victory in Jesus."*

X-TREME TEENS

JOSEPH
GENESIS 37:2

Joseph was betrayed by his own brothers and sold into slavery. He even faced immoral temptation and was thrown into prison. These events happened to him as a teenager. Just like Joseph, we as Christians face temptation and overcome it in our lives and come out Better.

SAMSON
JUDGES 13:24

Although Samson made some mistakes he did accomplish much for God. If we are going to accomplish anything for Christ, we are going to need th Holy Spirit of God that often rested on Samson. Teenager, the power of th Holy Spirit is not just for a preacher or an aged saint, it is for you! To be a better Christian, you will need to be filled with the Holy Spirit.

THREE HEBREWS BOYS
DANIEL 3:1

Shadrach, Meshach, and Abed-nego, stood for what was right when all others did not. Although every one in the audience bowed down to the idol, they stood for God. They refused to bow down to idolatry, peer pressure and compromise. They had been away from home for a long time and could have tried to fit in with the crowd, but instead they stood tall for God. To be better you will need to stand for Christ in the world.

JONATHAN
1 SAMUEL 18:1

Jonathan teaches us how to be a true friend. We as teenagers need to be careful who we chose to be our friends. Show me your friends and I wil show you who you will become. You should have friends that love God, and that want to serve Him. Be careful about spending time with those tha misbehave in church and, disrespect the things of God. Jonathan was a good influence on David. What type of friend are you, and what type of friends do you have? Be a better friend. Have better friends.

X-TREME TEENS

UZZIAH

2 CHRONICLES 26:3

Uzziah took over the kingdom at just seventeen years old. It would of been the popular thing to do to just follow the culture and continue doing wrong. But as a teenager Uzziah chose to do right in a wicked environment. As teenagers you might think you can not live for Jesus or be pure with all the wickedness that you see or hear but you can.

JOSHUA

EXODUS 33:11

Joshua was a servant. .Before before he led the children of Israel out of the wilderness, around Jericho to defeat the enemy he was a servant As teenagers we need to learn to just be a servant for Jesus Christ. Before you can be a leader in the youth department you need to be a servant. Before you become a pastor you need to learn to clean a bathroom Be faithful in those few things and God can use you in the many. Be better at being being a servant.

TIMOTHY

1 TIMOTHY 4:12

This verse is talking about living in such a way as a young person that no one canlook at your life anddespise your teen years. Instead he wants you to be an example to the adults. The adults should look at the teenagers in your church and want to serve God because they see your desire to serve God as a youth department. Be Better at your testimony.

X-TREME TEENS

DAVID

1 SAMUEL 17:20
David was a shepherd. He had a job as a teenager. He got up early. He took care of responsibility. He played an instrument. He obeyed his parents. He cared for his brothers. He loved his country. All of this is found in chapter 17 before he kills Goliath. David was more than just a giant killer. He was had character. Character beats talent when talent doesn't work.

DANIEL

DANIEL 1:8
Daniel was just a teenager when he was kidnapped and taken from his home. He could of simply done wrong and no one would of ever known at all. Daniel would of never lived for God in Babylon if he at first would of never lived for God in Judah. He wouldn't have prayed three times a day in Babylon if he didn't do it in Judah. Do right when no one is around. That is called integrity. Be better.

JESUS

LUKE 2:40
As a Christian we should always be growing I find it interesting that even Jesus himself found it important to grow. Of course Jesus himself did not need to grow because he was God. But as a man he did, Jesus is teaching us that we need to grow as christians. We should be better. Our goal is not our neighbor or friend. Our goal is to conform to the image of Christ. We should strive to be better until we are fully like Jesus.

THE X COMMANDMENTS

EXODUS 20:1-17 & DEUTERONOMY 5:6-21

1. THOU SHALT HAVE NO OTHER gods BEFORE ME
2. THOU SHALT NOT MAKE UNTO THEE ANY GRAVEN IMAGE
3. THOU SHALT NOT TAKE THE NAME OF THE LORD THY GOD IN VAIN
4. REMEMBER THE SABBATH DAY SUN MON TUES WED THU FRI SAT TO KEEP IT HOLY
5. HONOR THY FATHER and THY MOTHER
6. THOU SHALT NOT KILL
7. THOU SHALT NOT COMMIT ADULTERY
8. THOU SHALT NOT STEAL
9. THOU SHALT NOT BEAR FALSE WITNESS
10. THOU SHALT NOT COVET

THOU SHALT LOVE THE **LORD THY GOD** WITH *ALL* THY **HEART** and WITH *ALL* THY **SOUL** and WITH *ALL* THY **MIND** THIS IS THE FIRST and **GREAT COMMANDMENT**

THE SECOND IS LIKE UNTO IT **THOU SHALT LOVE** *thy* **NEIGHBOR** AS THYSELF ON THESE TWO **COMMANDMENTS** HANG ALL THE LAW and **THE PROPHETS**

(MATTHEW 22:37-40 KJV)

-PRAYER LIST-

SUNDAY

REQUESTS		DATE ANSWERED
1.	PASTOR	
2.	YP	
3.	S.S. TEACHER	
4.	BUS CAPTAIN	
5.	CHURCH	
6.	VISITORS	
7.	SOULS	
8.	POWER	
9.	WISDOM	
10.	MIND OF CHRIST	

PRAYER LIST

MONDAY

REQUESTS	DATE ANSWERED
1. THANKFUL FOR MY SALVATION	
2. THANKFUL FOR AMERICA	
3. THANKFUL FOR GOD'S BLESSINGS	
4. THANKFUL FOR ANSWERED PRAYER	
5. THANKFUL FOR MY CHURCH	
6. THANKFUL FOR GOD'S WORD	
7. SOULS	
8. POWER	
9. WISDOM	
10. MIND OF CHRIST	

PRAYER LIST

TUESDAY

REQUESTS	DATE ANSWERED
1. PRESIDENT	
2. ELECTED OFFICIALS	
3. MILITARY	
4. POLICE / FIRE FIGHTERS / EMS	
5. ISRAEL	
6. NATIONAL REVIVAL	
7. SOULS	
8. POWER	
9. WISDOM	
10. MIND OF CHRIST	

PRAYER LIST

WEDNESDAY

REQUESTS	DATE ANSWERED
1. YOUTH GROUP	
2. TEEN SOUL-WINNING	
3. CHURCH	
4. FRIENDS	
5. STRUGGLING CHRISTIANS	
6. PERSONAL NEEDS	
7. SOULS	
8. POWER	
9. WISDOM	
10. MIND OF CHRIST	

PRAYER LIST

THURSDAY

REQUESTS		DATE ANSWERED
1.	MISSIONARIES	
2.	CAMP	
3.	COLLEGE	
4.	SCHOOL	
5.	PASTOR	
6.	EVANGELISTS	
7.	SOULS	
8.	POWER	
9.	WISDOM	
10.	MIND OF CHRIST	
•		
•		
•		
•		
•		
•		
•		
•		
•		
•		
•		
•		
•		
•		
•		
•		
•		
•		

PRAYER LIST

FRIDAY

REQUESTS		DATE ANSWERED
1. **PARENTS**		
2. **SIBLINGS**		
3. **EXTENDED FAMILY**		
4. **LOST LOVED ONES**		
5. **FRIENDS**		
6. **SICK**		
7. **SOULS**		
8. **POWER**		
9. **WISDOM**		
10. **MIND OF CHRIST**		
•		
•		
•		
•		
•		
•		
•		
•		
•		
•		
•		
•		
•		
•		
•		
•		
•		

– PRAYER LIST –

SATURDAY

REQUESTS	DATE ANSWERED
1. BUS KIDS	
2. VISITATION	
3. SOUL-WINNERS	
4. CHURCH MINISTRIES	
5. MINISTRY LEADERS	
6. CITY WIDE REVIVAL	
7. SOULS	
8. POWER	
9. WISDOM	
10. MIND OF CHRIST	

X WAYS TO GET THE MOST OUT OF CHURCH

1. **BRING YOUR BIBLE**
2. **DRESS UP**
3. **BE FRIENDLY**
4. **SIT IN THE FRONT**
5. **SING**
6. **GIVE**
7. **PRAY FOR THE PASTOR**
8. **LISTEN**
9. **TAKE NOTES**
10. **USE THE ALTAR**

-William Davis

SERMON NOTES

TITLE Serving God
PREACHER Jim Jorgensen   **DATE** 3-17-9
TEXT Daniel 2:8   **SERVICE** NyFc(x)

I don't control me God does. We need to surrender to God.

SERMON NOTES

TITLE We need a seeker 4 your generation
PREACHER Justin Cooper   **DATE** 3-17-19
TEXT II Chronicles 26:1-5   **SERVICE** NYFC(?)

If God can use Uzziah he can use you. We don't kneed more boys we need more young men. How much longer will have freedom. Will you be a seeker for your church? God wants us to seek him. The seeker makes the difference. God is 10GI times better than anything in this world.

-SERMON NOTES-

TITLE _____

PREACHER _____ DATE _____

TEXT _____ SERVICE _____

_____
_____
_____
_____
_____
_____
_____
_____
_____
_____
_____
_____
_____
_____
_____
_____
_____
_____
_____
_____
_____
_____
_____
_____
_____
_____
_____
_____
_____

-SERMON NOTES-

TITLE _____
PREACHER _____ DATE _____
TEXT _____ SERVICE _____

SERMON NOTES

TITLE _____

PREACHER _____ **DATE** _____

TEXT _____ **SERVICE** ____

-SERMON NOTES-

TITLE_____

PREACHER_____ DATE_____

TEXT_____ SERVICE_____

-SERMON NOTES-

TITLE _____

PREACHER _____ **DATE** _____

TEXT _____ **SERVICE** _____

-SERMON NOTES-

TITLE_____

PREACHER_____ DATE_____

TEXT_____ SERVICE_____

_____
_____
_____
_____
_____
_____
_____
_____
_____
_____
_____
_____
_____
_____
_____
_____
_____
_____
_____
_____
_____
_____
_____
_____
_____
_____
_____
_____
_____
_____

-SERMON NOTES-

TITLE_____

PREACHER_____ **DATE**_____

TEXT_____ **SERVICE**_____

-SERMON NOTES-

TITLE _____

PREACHER _____ DATE _____

TEXT _____ SERVICE _____

_____
_____
_____
_____
_____
_____
_____
_____
_____
_____
_____
_____
_____
_____
_____
_____
_____
_____
_____
_____
_____
_____
_____
_____
_____
_____
_____
_____

-SERMON NOTES-

TITLE _____
PREACHER _____ **DATE** _____
TEXT _____ **SERVICE** _____

-SERMON NOTES-

TITLE _____
PREACHER _____ DATE _____
TEXT _____ SERVICE _____

SERMON NOTES

TITLE _____

PREACHER _____ **DATE** _____

TEXT _____ **SERVICE** _____

_____
_____
_____
_____
_____
_____
_____
_____
_____
_____
_____
_____
_____
_____
_____
_____
_____
_____
_____
_____
_____
_____
_____
_____
_____
_____
_____
_____
_____

-SERMON NOTES-

TITLE _____
PREACHER _____ DATE _____
TEXT _____ SERVICE _____

-SERMON NOTES-

TITLE _____
PREACHER _____ **DATE** _____
TEXT _____ **SERVICE** _____

_____
_____
_____
_____
_____
_____
_____
_____
_____
_____
_____
_____
_____
_____
_____
_____
_____
_____
_____
_____
_____
_____
_____
_____
_____
_____
_____
_____
_____

SERMON NOTES

TITLE _____

PREACHER _____ DATE _____

TEXT _____ SERVICE _____

-SERMON NOTES-

TITLE _____

PREACHER _____ **DATE** _____

TEXT _____ **SERVICE** _____

_____
_____
_____
_____
_____
_____
_____
_____
_____
_____
_____
_____
_____
_____
_____
_____
_____
_____
_____
_____
_____
_____
_____
_____
_____
_____
_____

SERMON NOTES

TITLE _____

PREACHER _____ DATE _____

TEXT _____ SERVICE _____

-SERMON NOTES-

TITLE _____

PREACHER _____ **DATE** _____

TEXT _____ **SERVICE** _____

_____
_____
_____
_____
_____
_____
_____
_____
_____
_____
_____
_____
_____
_____
_____
_____
_____
_____
_____
_____
_____
_____
_____
_____
_____
_____
_____
_____
_____
_____

SERMON NOTES

TITLE _____

PREACHER _____ DATE _____

TEXT _____ SERVICE _____

SERMON NOTES

TITLE _____

PREACHER _____ **DATE** _____

TEXT _____ **SERVICE** _____

SERMON NOTES

TITLE _____

PREACHER _____ DATE _____

TEXT _____ SERVICE _____

-SERMON NOTES-

TITLE _____

PREACHER _____ **DATE** _____

TEXT _____ **SERVICE** _____

-SERMON NOTES-

TITLE _____
PREACHER _____ DATE _____
TEXT _____ SERVICE _____

-SERMON NOTES-

TITLE _____

PREACHER _____ **DATE** _____

TEXT _____ **SERVICE** _____

_____
_____
_____
_____
_____
_____
_____
_____
_____
_____
_____
_____
_____
_____
_____
_____
_____
_____
_____
_____
_____
_____
_____
_____
_____
_____
_____
_____
_____

SERMON NOTES

TITLE _____
PREACHER _____ DATE _____
TEXT _____ SERVICE _____

_____
_____
_____
_____
_____
_____
_____
_____
_____
_____
_____
_____
_____
_____
_____
_____
_____
_____
_____
_____
_____
_____
_____
_____
_____
_____
_____
_____
_____
_____
_____

-SERMON NOTES-

TITLE _____
PREACHER _____ **DATE** _____
TEXT _____ **SERVICE** _____

-SERMON NOTES-

TITLE _____
PREACHER _____ DATE _____
TEXT _____ SERVICE _____

_____
_____
_____
_____
_____
_____
_____
_____
_____
_____
_____
_____
_____
_____
_____
_____
_____
_____
_____
_____
_____
_____
_____
_____
_____
_____
_____
_____
_____
_____

-SERMON NOTES-

TITLE _____

PREACHER _____ **DATE** _____

TEXT _____ **SERVICE** _____

-SERMON NOTES-

TITLE _____
PREACHER _____ DATE _____
TEXT _____ SERVICE _____

-SERMON NOTES-

TITLE _____
PREACHER _____ DATE _____
TEXT _____ SERVICE _____

_____
_____
_____
_____
_____
_____
_____
_____
_____
_____
_____
_____
_____
_____
_____
_____
_____
_____
_____
_____
_____
_____
_____
_____
_____
_____

-SERMON NOTES-

TITLE _____
PREACHER _____ **DATE** _____
TEXT _____ **SERVICE** _____

-SERMON NOTES-

TITLE _____

PREACHER _____ **DATE** _____

TEXT _____ **SERVICE** _____

_____
_____
_____
_____
_____
_____
_____
_____
_____
_____
_____
_____
_____
_____
_____
_____
_____
_____
_____
_____
_____
_____
_____
_____
_____
_____
_____

SERMON NOTES

TITLE _____

PREACHER _____ DATE _____

TEXT _____ SERVICE _____

-SERMON NOTES-

TITLE _____

PREACHER _____ **DATE** _____

TEXT _____ **SERVICE** _____

-SERMON NOTES-

TITLE_____
PREACHER_____ DATE_____
TEXT_____ SERVICE_____

_____
_____
_____
_____
_____
_____
_____
_____
_____
_____
_____
_____
_____
_____
_____
_____
_____
_____
_____
_____
_____
_____
_____
_____
_____
_____
_____
_____
_____
_____
_____
_____
_____

-SERMON NOTES-

TITLE _____

PREACHER _____ **DATE** _____

TEXT _____ **SERVICE** _____

SERMON NOTES

TITLE _____

PREACHER _____ DATE _____

TEXT _____ SERVICE _____

-SERMON NOTES-

TITLE _____

PREACHER _____ **DATE** _____

TEXT _____ **SERVICE** _____

_____
_____
_____
_____
_____
_____
_____
_____
_____
_____
_____
_____
_____
_____
_____
_____
_____
_____
_____
_____
_____
_____
_____
_____
_____
_____
_____
_____
_____
_____

-SERMON NOTES-

TITLE _____

PREACHER _____ **DATE** _____

TEXT _____ **SERVICE** _____

-SERMON NOTES-

TITLE _____

PREACHER _____ **DATE** _____

TEXT _____ **SERVICE** _____

-SERMON NOTES-

TITLE _____
PREACHER _____ DATE _____
TEXT _____ SERVICE _____

-SERMON NOTES-

TITLE _____

PREACHER _____ **DATE** _____

TEXT _____ **SERVICE** _____

_____
_____
_____
_____
_____
_____
_____
_____
_____
_____
_____
_____
_____
_____
_____
_____
_____
_____
_____
_____
_____
_____
_____
_____
_____
_____
_____
_____
_____

-SERMON NOTES-

TITLE _____
PREACHER _____ DATE _____
TEXT _____ SERVICE _____

-SERMON NOTES-

TITLE _____

PREACHER _____ **DATE** _____

TEXT _____ **SERVICE** ____

SERMON NOTES

TITLE _____

PREACHER _____ DATE _____

TEXT _____ SERVICE _____

-SERMON NOTES-

TITLE _____

PREACHER _____ **DATE** _____

TEXT _____ **SERVICE** _____

SERMON NOTES

TITLE _____

PREACHER _____ DATE _____

TEXT _____ SERVICE _____

_____
_____
_____
_____
_____
_____
_____
_____
_____
_____
_____
_____
_____
_____
_____
_____
_____
_____
_____
_____
_____
_____
_____
_____
_____
_____
_____
_____

-SERMON NOTES-

TITLE _____
PREACHER _____ **DATE** _____
TEXT _____ **SERVICE** _____

SERMON NOTES

TITLE _____
PREACHER _____ DATE _____
TEXT _____ SERVICE _____

-SERMON NOTES-

TITLE _____

PREACHER _____ **DATE** _____

TEXT _____ **SERVICE** _____

_____
_____
_____
_____
_____
_____
_____
_____
_____
_____
_____
_____
_____
_____
_____
_____
_____
_____
_____
_____
_____
_____
_____
_____
_____
_____
_____
_____

-SERMON NOTES-

TITLE: _____
PREACHER: _____ DATE: _____
TEXT: _____ SERVICE: _____

MONTH:

SUNDAY	MONDAY	TUESDAY	WEDNESDAY	THURSDAY	FRIDAY	SATURDAY

TEN TIMES BETTER

MONTH:

SUNDAY	MONDAY	TUESDAY	WEDNESDAY	THURSDAY	FRIDAY	SATURDAY

TEN TIMES BETTER

MONTH:

SUNDAY	MONDAY	TUESDAY	WEDNESDAY	THURSDAY	FRIDAY	SATURDAY

TEN TIMES BETTER

MONTH:

SUNDAY	MONDAY	TUESDAY	WEDNESDAY	THURSDAY	FRIDAY	SATURDAY

TEN TIMES BETTER

MONTH:

SUNDAY	MONDAY	TUESDAY	WEDNESDAY	THURSDAY	FRIDAY	SATURDAY

TEN TIMES BETTER

MONTH:

SUNDAY	MONDAY	TUESDAY	WEDNESDAY	THURSDAY	FRIDAY	SATURDAY

TEN TIMES BETTER

MONTH:

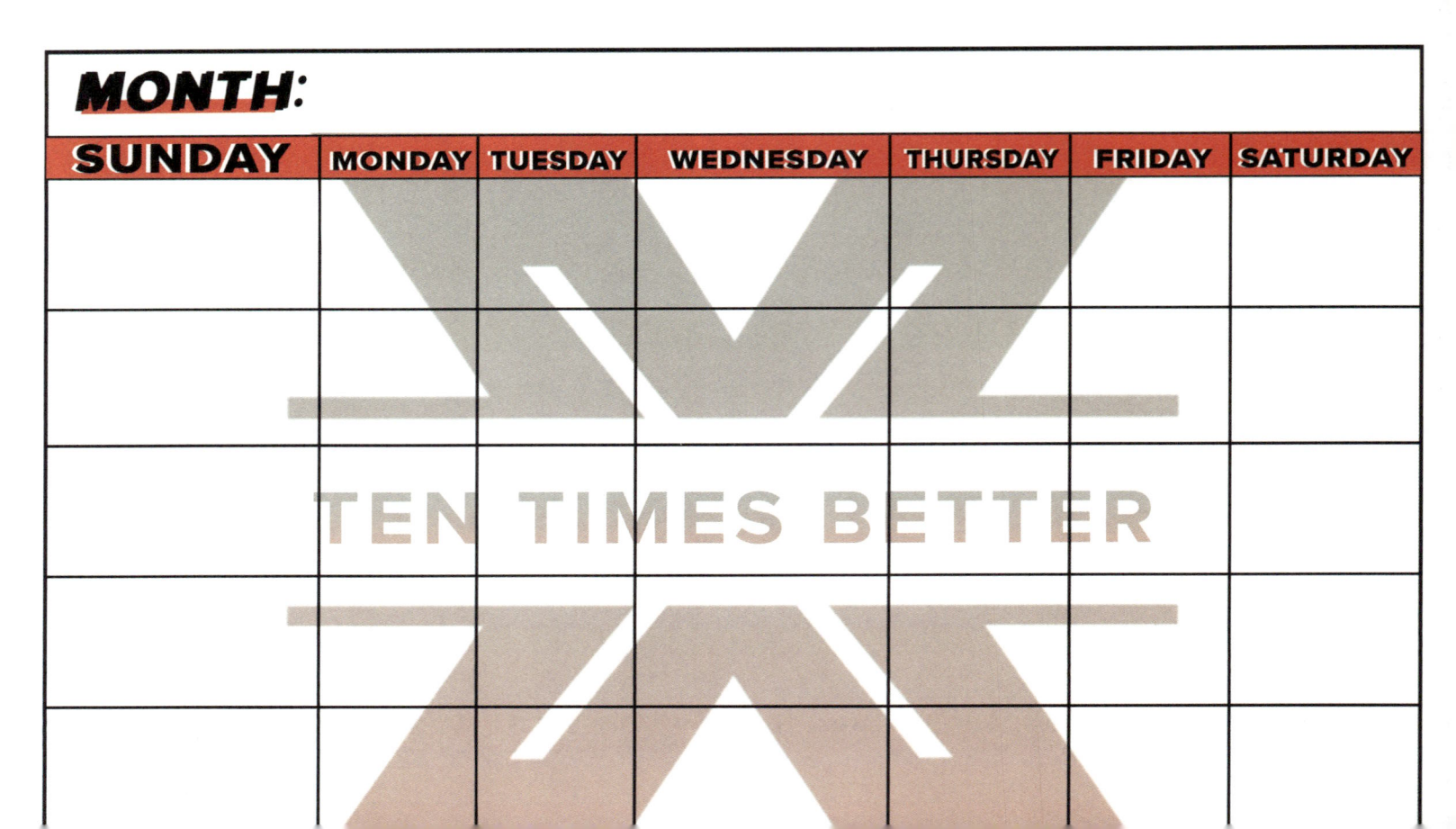

SUNDAY	MONDAY	TUESDAY	WEDNESDAY	THURSDAY	FRIDAY	SATURDAY

TEN TIMES BETTER

MONTH:

SUNDAY	MONDAY	TUESDAY	WEDNESDAY	THURSDAY	FRIDAY	SATURDAY

TEN TIMES BETTER

MONTH:

SUNDAY	MONDAY	TUESDAY	WEDNESDAY	THURSDAY	FRIDAY	SATURDAY

TEN TIMES BETTER

MONTH:

SUNDAY	MONDAY	TUESDAY	WEDNESDAY	THURSDAY	FRIDAY	SATURDAY

TEN TIMES BETTER

MONTH:

SUNDAY	MONDAY	TUESDAY	WEDNESDAY	THURSDAY	FRIDAY	SATURDAY

TEN TIMES BETTER

MONTH:

SUNDAY	MONDAY	TUESDAY	WEDNESDAY	THURSDAY	FRIDAY	SATURDAY
			TEN TIMES BETTER			

CLASSIC
CHALLENGING
CONSISTENT
CONSERVATIVE
COMMONWEALTH

MAKE PLANS TO ATTEND:

- INDEPENDENT FINE ARTS COMPETITION
- COLLEGE DAYS

COMMONWEATLH BAPTIST COLLEGE | COMMONNWEALTH BAPTIST.ORG | 1.877.682.8318

THE PLAYBOOK
A 365 DAY GAMEPLAN FOR WINNING THE CHRISTIAN LIFE.

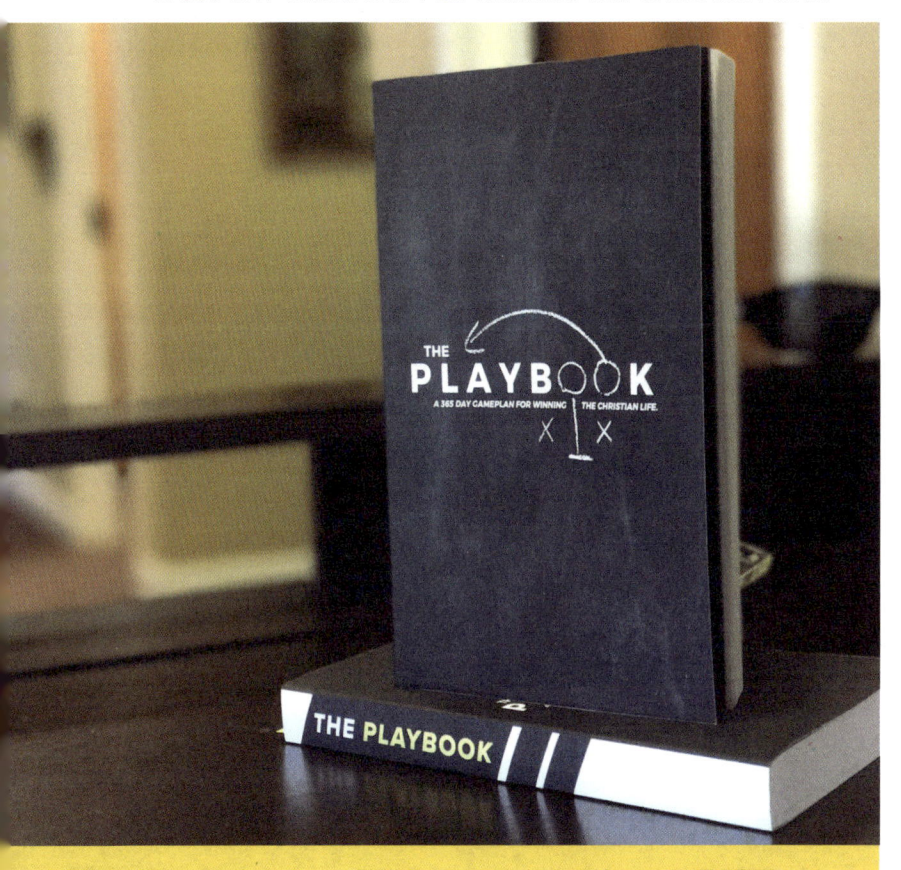

The Playbook is a 365 page devotional **JUST FOR TEENS.** Written by some of the finest pastors, and youth pastors in America, and across the world. The Playbook is available for purchase for only $10.

AVAILABLE NOW AT YPSTORE.ORG

ALL BOOKS AVAILABLE at ⬇ YPLIFE.ORG

Works of the Holy Spirit
PASTOR CARL HATMAKER
$5

The Captain's Log
$5
A 52 WEEK GUIDE FOR SAILING THE SEAS OF A SPIRITUAL LIFE

From High School to High Calling
EXPERIENCING GOD'S PLAN IN AN UNCERTAIN TIME
$5
SAM GECKLER

visit YPLIFE.ORG

CATEGORIES FEATURING:

- 4 the YP
- Youth Truth
- YP Wife
- YP Games
- YP Activities

X *TIMES BETTER*
BULK PRICES

10 BOOKS: $5 EACH

20 BOOKS: $4.50 EACH

30 BOOKS: $4.50 EACH

40 BOOKS: $4.50 EACH

50 BOOKS: $4 EACH

Shipping prices not included

to order, visit ypstore.org